VAMPIRES

VAMPIRES

Joules Taylor

spruce

Dedication

For Ferdinand, the pipistrelle that haunts our garden; for bats the world over; and for those who work for their conservation.

An Hachette UK Company
First published in Great Britain in 2009 by Spruce
a division of Octopus Publishing Group Ltd
2–4 Heron Quays, London E14 4JP
www.octopusbooks.co.uk
www.octopusbooksusa.com

Distributed in the U.S. and Canada for
Octopus Books USA
Hachette Book Group USA
237 Park Avenue
New York NY 10017

Produced by **Bookworx**
Editor: Jo Godfrey Wood, Designer: Peggy Sadler
Editorial assistant: Hannah Eiseman-Renyard

ISBN 13 978-1-84601-345-4
ISBN 10 1-84601-345-3

A CIP catalog record for this book is available from the British Library.

Printed and bound in China

10 9 8 7 6 5 4 3 2 1

CONTENTS

Introduction

Dark, brooding, and seductive, the image of the vampire haunts the modern consciousness, a temptation to give in to the darkness that dwells within us all. At its simplest, a vampire is a reanimated, soulless, dead human who must drink the blood of others to remain "alive." But the simplest answer hardly scratches the surface of what a vampire actually is.

Originally a thing of fear and disgust, little by little the vampire grew to be seen as a tragic figure, lonely and often misunderstood, but nevertheless powerful and possessing an unearthly, if not always conventional, physical beauty. His supernatural strength and speed, his enhanced hearing and vision and seeming telepathic abilities intensify his already potent attraction. Add to this his considerable charm and charisma, his elegance, his skills in enthralling and captivating his prey: all the things that make him so darkly, so deliciously hot, and who wouldn't want to be noticed, to be courted, by such a being?

A DIET OF NOTHING BUT BLOOD

Yet the vampire isn't perfect, nor is he indestructible. He has traded a normal human life for immortality, the savors of human existence for the life of a predator and a diet of nothing but blood. He's a rebel, an individual at odds with the mundane, often boring, nature of human life, forced to deal with all the trials and problems that such a life normally entails, along with the fact that he's no longer truly human. Much like any rebel, life, or rather "undeath" in the vampire's case, isn't easy. Do the benefits outweigh the disadvantages? Given the choice, who would opt for a vampire's life? For those who feel they don't belong, the dispossessed, the alien, the unconventional, or even for those simply looking for some excitement in their life, it has a deep emotional fascination.

A BEAUTIFUL SOUL

Bella, the love-struck narrator of *Twilight*, a book by Stephenie Meyer that was made into this film, describes vampire Edward Cullen like this: "He had the most beautiful soul, more beautiful than his brilliant mind or his incomparable face or his glorious body."

RECOGNIZING YOUR VAMPIRE

Traditionally, it was easy to spot a vampire. Pale, often plump from all the blood they'd drunk, and unpleasantly smelly from both their diet and from sleeping in a coffin, they would recoil from a cross, crucifix, holy water, or garlic, were unable to cross water or go onto consecrated ground, threw no reflection in a mirror or mirrored surface, could not enter a building unless they were invited in, and burned in sunlight. They were able to shape-shift into a wolf or bat, or into a mist that could seep under doors and through keyholes in order to gain access to their prey, and they could control certain animals as well: wolves, bats, and rats, and have the beasts do their bidding. Some could fly in their human form, and could climb walls and ceilings like a spider. They weren't too difficult to spot, if you knew what you were looking for!

Now, however, the situation is different. The vampire has evolved from the monster of old into something that is much less obvious, much more able to blend into human civilization. It's a survival tactic, of course: we are a little less primitive, but humans still have a tendency to attack or want to destroy what they don't understand, or what they perceive as a threat, so passing for human is an altogether much safer tactic. Society is, to a large extent, more egalitarian, too: the days of automatic obedience to the nobility are gone, and trying to lord it over one's fellow human being is more likely to produce a mouthful of abuse or a swift kick than a bow and a tug of the forelock.

There is still an emphasis on darkness, however. The vampire is a thing of darkness, after all, dying from human life to rise to immortal undeath. Even if, as was traditionally the case and is still portrayed in some examples of the species, the vampire can endure sunlight (even if he doesn't particularly like it), he is usually pallid except immediately after a meal, when he may be quite rosy and human-looking. The night is his natural time: he is adapted to it, his vision and often his senses are of more use to him in the darkness, when the human world is half-blind and sleeping.

The modern vampire possesses more than human strength and speed, and an otherworldly glamor that sets him apart from humans. Since he's pretty much invulnerable to anything except a stake through the heart, decapitation, or, often, sunlight, he usually has a devil-may-care attitude to life, a casual manner toward danger that can be very appealing to humans who have to be careful of injury. His uncanny ability to anticipate human thoughts, and charm those around him, add to his charisma. Are vampires telepathic? It would seem many, if not all, modern vampires possess the ability. It may be a hangover from ancient times when the skill was useful to call his human servants, his thralls, to him at need. These days it's more useful to keep a check on those around him, in case of danger or threat. Or to seduce, of course. It's far easier to attract prey if you can "read" what the other finds erotic and deliver it to them. It makes them far more willing, and often happy to "donate" on other occasions.

> "Why are we always insanely attracted to the bad boy?"
>
> Vicki Nelson, *Blood Ties*, Episode Nine, *Stone Cold*

Today's vampire has chosen not to be human. Turning his back on human morality, society, and mortality, he has deliberately become something "other"; something more than human. Whatever we feel about his morals or his choice, we can't help but admire him for having the strength and determination to make that choice in the first place.

This book is an attempt to explore the subject of vampirism, showing how it originated, what it has meant to us in centuries past, and what it has come to mean to us in the modern world.

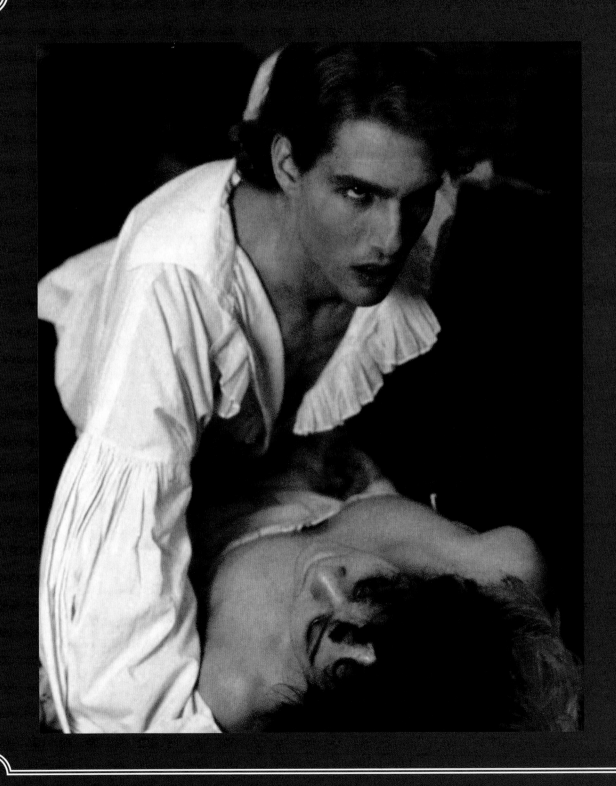

Chapter 1

Vampires:
Body & Soul

Why We all Love Vampires

Why is it that we humans find vampires so deeply fascinating? In the early days of our history and development it was their gruesomeness that we loved so much; the stuff that made the shivers run up and down our spines. This caused vampires to become part of our fatal fascination (we all love a good horror story; it gets our adrenalin flowing and our blood pumping like a fairground ride).

The forbidden and the tragic

Later on in our human history we found that we were tantalized by what we weren't allowed to have. Isn't it true that what we can't do always seems so much more exciting and tempting? We always want what we can't have; it seems to be part of who we are as human beings. Then we began to see the vampire as a bit of a tragic figure; he was lonely and alone, unable to make friends or to have a family, doomed never to walk around in the sunshine, see beautiful flowers in daylight or feel the love of a child. For some women, the urge to play mom to this poor tortured soul would be irresistible.

The charm of "otherness"

As our fascination grew, it was the "otherness" of the vampire that we, his fans, loved; he seemed excitingly different and remote. For anyone who felt like being rebellious, the vampire was a terrific role model. Romantic and stylish, being a vampire means being free from all the usual conventions. He lives outside normal society. But perhaps, most of all, it's his aloneness, away from other beings, that makes him so attractive to so many people. Anyone who feels as though they're an outcast themselves, lonely and friendless in an increasingly complicated world, sees the vampire as a fellow sufferer, a kindred spirit; a symbol to hold on to when life gets too much to bear.

THE LOVER FROM THE DARK

We humans may have brightened up the dark night with our torches and streetlamps, but beyond the range of that friendly yellow glow we can never be sure what's watching us from dark corners. This is because the vampire is a usually a hunter; an expert predator, like a python. He feels drawn to life, to brightness, and to beauty and the human he pursues must be someone who is special, overflowing with a bright, lively energy.

The right moment

Driven by his deep need, the vampire lurks in the dark, out of sight, choosing his prey with care. He then stalks her, woos her, and charms her before making her his own. It's an intense and tormented relationship. He depends on her for his survival, to provide him with the nourishment he needs (he needs both her blood and her love), and for a way to experience at second-hand the life he lost when he became a vampire. Enchanted by his beauty and his power, his victim learns to depend on him for support and protection, and loves knowing how much she means to him.

A love that lasts

The love of a vampire goes on forever, but the life of a human being is all too short. So the vampire must choose; should he make his loved one into one of his own species, condemned to a dark, sometimes lonely, life witnessing her own friends and family die or have to watch, in anguish, as she eventually withers and dies. It's little wonder that he can't resist the temptation to make her his soulmate, to enjoy the wonders of life as the

A BEAUTIFUL RELATIONSHIP

In this still from *Twilight* of Bella and Edward at the prom, Bella is already certain of her desire to join Edward in "undeath." Although Edward is desperately tempted to make her his own, he hesitates, because he doesn't want her to later regret missing out on having a human life.

centuries pass by, and this feeling usually wins out. Imagine, for a moment, having endless time to play in, as well as a lovely immortal one to share it with...

It's a tempting idea, to both the vampire and the human, so tempting, in fact, that the human may not want to confront the things that will change when she becomes a vampire: she will lose the daylight world and have a perpetual need to hunt, plus be immortal. Because, of course, she will have to face up to the same choices and dilemmas once she becomes undead herself.

PATHS TO DARKNESS

Becoming a vampire can be difficult. In the old days it was enough to have committed suicide (and hope for the best, since people thought that suicide victims could also come back as ghosts or ghouls if they were particularly unlucky).

The fate of suicides

The Church believed that suicide, when a person kills himself, was the taking away of a precious life given by God by the very person who had been so blessed by Him. This was thought to be a truly unforgivable sin and these people could not be buried in sacred ground; their bodies couldn't decay and so their souls were lost for all time.

Meanwhile these unfortunates' physical shells, in some cases possessed by a demon, rose from their graves in unconsecrated ground to roam the night, preying miserably on the living, whose souls were still capable of being saved and going to Heaven.

Cruel lives

People who had led especially cruel or violent lives, or who had been corrupt, could also come back as vampires after their death, because people thought that they were too bad, their souls too wicked, to be welcomed into Heaven. Death by drowning or some other violent, lonely death, or if someone's murder had not been avenged, all carried a risk, unfair as it was, of the victim being forced to join the ranks of the undead.

Unfortunate births

But, of course, there were many other ways to become a vampire. Children whose parents weren't married and whose parents before them hadn't been married either, were said to become vampires after death, as were children born at unlucky times; usually during Church holy days such as Christmas or Easter. The children of witches, too, were prime candidates for vampirehood after their deaths. Fortunately, as the Church gradually lost its authority and a deeper understanding of human nature developed, with today's more tolerant attitudes such beliefs have faded. We now have few reasons to worry about any religious or spiritual consequences of not toeing the Church line.

Being "turned"

The most usual method of becoming one of the undead is to be "turned," or transformed, by another vampire. There are several ways for this to be achieved. It isn't absolutely necessary for a vampire to kill his victim: the modern vampire does not actually need a body's-worth of blood to fill him up each time, even if he could stomach it.

The healthy adult human body contains, on average, five liters (ten and a half pints) of blood, and can lose fifteen percent of the total volume with no lasting ill-effects (so all those vampire films that show the victim dying after losing just a few drops of blood are probably exaggerating to make the film seem more exciting, unless, of course, their victim's death was caused by shock). However, if the vampire does kill his prey, the victim will rise from the dead as a vampire, under the control of the one who made her, until either he gives up control or the newly raised vampire gains enough power to break free.

Just drinking

Another tradition states that even if the vampire doesn't kill his victims outright, but simply drinks from them, they will still become vampires when they die. The number of times it's necessary for the vampire to feed from his prey before this becomes inevitable varies from once to many times, with an option that he may continue to feed until his victim wastes away and dies. There is one very obvious problem with this: if every victim of a vampire becomes a vampire in their turn, being immortal and needing to feed, the world would be hip-deep in vampires in no time at all; metaphorically speaking, of course!

The third way

The third method to be turned is both the most dramatic and the most sensible: the victim must drink the vampire's blood in order to become one themselves. This is the tradition you will see if you watch films such as *Dracula* and read Anne Rice's *Vampire Chronicles*. It also presents vampirehood

Types of Vampire

 Although traditionally the term "revenant" (French for "returning," as in returning from the grave) is used for all vampires, it is useful here to distinguish between the two main types of vampire: the almost mindless revenant, driven by its appetite for blood and death, and the true vampire, who still possesses his human social skills, intelligence, and a remnant of conscience. Although both are driven by the need for blood to survive, the first kind is far from appealing, while the latter might be very appealing indeed. While the revenant will usually kill its prey, causing great pain and terror, it isn't necessary for this to happen. It is, after all, not a good idea to draw attention to yourself by leaving a lot of bloodless corpses lying around for other people to find...

as a gift that is given deliberately and consciously, rather than simply a side effect of a vampire's feeding. This is a much more appropriate bequest because, let's be honest, immortality, even under such conditions, shouldn't be something that is granted without a lot of thought. However, the most well-known way of becoming a vampire is to be bitten by one; to die at the hands and teeth of one of the undead.

THE DARK KISS

Eyes may be the doorway into our souls, but mouths provide the stuff of life. From the moment we are born we grow strong by drinking our mother's milk, and show our love for each other through kissing. Our sensitive lips, our teeth, and our tongues give us great pleasure. They're also most likely to be our main way of communicating with each other, through speech.

The vampire's mouth

For the vampire the mouth is even more important than it is for humans. Because he is unable to show normal physical affection to someone, he has to use his lips and tongue. The way he communicates physically is made up of kisses, touches, and bites.

Showing feelings

Depending on how deep his feelings are for his prey and how much he needs her blood, he can be a tender lover or more intense and passionate. If his need is less desperate, or if he really does love his victim, he will be gentle and ardent, drinking only enough to keep himself alive.

THE PERFECT SPOT →

In *Taste the Blood of Dracula*, the movie made in 1969 starring Christopher Lee, the vampire opts for the classic bite location: the tender, sensitive place where the neck and body join.

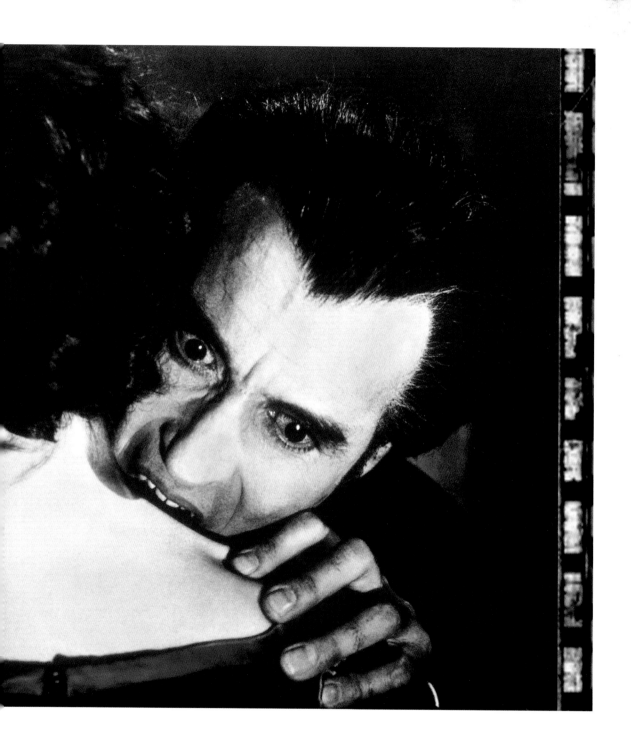

Vampire Characteristics

 NO REFLECTION

Primitive peoples have often believed that mirrors or reflective surfaces give back an image of the soul: the notion that led to the superstition that having one's photo taken stole part of that soul. It was only a short step to believing that a vampire, who traditionally lacks a soul, has no reflection. In later times it was proposed that it was the silver that backed mirrors that did not capture a vampire's reflection, silver being a magical and pure metal, but that their reflection could be seen in still water. Leading on from this is the idea that the image of the vampire cannot be captured by anything involving silver such as photographic film.

SUPERNATURALLY FAST HEALING

Usually this requires a meal of blood, but once that need has been fulfilled, the most deadly wounds are able to heal while the vampire rests during the day—with a few obvious exceptions: even a vampire can't recover from decapitation, or from burning to ash after having its heart removed. Staking may not be secure, as an old and experienced vampire may be able to remove the stake before it can inflict fatal damage, or it may be removed by other means and the body rejuvenated by blood. Staking was originally meant simply to prevent the vampire getting out of its coffin, not necessarily to kill it.

HYPNOTIC PERSONALITY

The vampire's ability to hypnotize his victims makes it much easier for him to feed, whether because he can force his prey to forget the encounter, or because he can make them believe that it was their own choice. This latter idea means the victim is extremely unlikely to accuse his attacker of any wrong-doing, no matter how uneasy he feels about the event!

VAMPIRES AND ANIMALS

Most animals, recognizing a predator, are uneasy when a vampire is near, especially the herbivores. Indeed, white horses were one of the means used to confirm whether someone was a vampire: if the horse refused to walk over the grave it was a sure sign that one of the undead lay within. Other predators, especially wolves, reacted as any carnivore would to an intruder on its territory—with hostility. However, since some vampires could control wolves, fear was mixed in with the enmity. It seems, too, that dogs dislike the undead, possibly because they are protective of their humans and see the vampire as a threat. Or it may just be that they react like the wolves they once were.

There is no common tradition regarding vampires and cats, though since felines are wholly independent creatures we can imagine they'd either ignore the vampire or demand to be fed!

ALL FOUR-FOOTED THINGS

Rats, bats, and spiders—the only creatures that can bear to be near a vampire without balking. Wolves will do his bidding, although they don't like it. But the larger animals are likely to flee or try to attack—and the vampire's hypnotic skills don't usually work on non-humans.

The Bite of the Vampire

A vampire feeds by biting into its victim's flesh and drinking the blood. Most vampires are shown as having fangs, usually instead of their canine teeth, although both the way they look and how they are disguised varies. And there are many different conceptions of a vampire's fangs. The fangs may be erectile, like a viper's, and folded back against the roof of the mouth when not in use. They may also be retractile, like a cat's claws, sliding back into the jaw. From a survival point of view this is probably the most successful form, as the fangs are then hidden.

Different versions

The movie version of Dracula tends not to smile or open his mouth very widely, keeping his ever-present fangs hidden, whereas in the book he wears a long white moustache to hide his teeth.

The fangs belonging to Max Shreck, the actor of the 1920s *Nosferatu* movie fame, are his central incisors, which are long, sharp, and pointed, resembling a vampire bat's teeth. The vampires in *The Lost Boys* usually look perfectly human, but transform when they are hunting, their faces becoming more animal-like and their upper incisor teeth becoming fangs.

In *Blood Ties*, Henry Fitzroy's upper lateral incisors and upper canines turn into fangs, which would make for a firmer grip but otherwise leave the bitten area in a bit of a mess. Angel, in the *Buffy the Vampire Slayer* spin-off *Angel*, also transforms facially. He becomes threatening and ugly, with his lateral incisors turning into ferocious fangs.

> "The mouth, so far as I could see it under the heavy moustache, was fixed and rather cruel-looking, with peculiarly sharp white teeth: these protruded over the lips, whose remarkable ruddiness showed astonishing vitality for a man of his years. For the rest, his ears were pale and at the tops extremely pointed..."
>
> *Dracula*, Bram Stoker

THE FULL HORROR

In the movie *Nosferatu*, this version made in 1978, directed by Werner Herzog, actors Klaus Kinski and Isabelle Adjani strike classic vampire-film poses, displaying outstretched white neck, ghastly fangs; the full works for a great horror film.

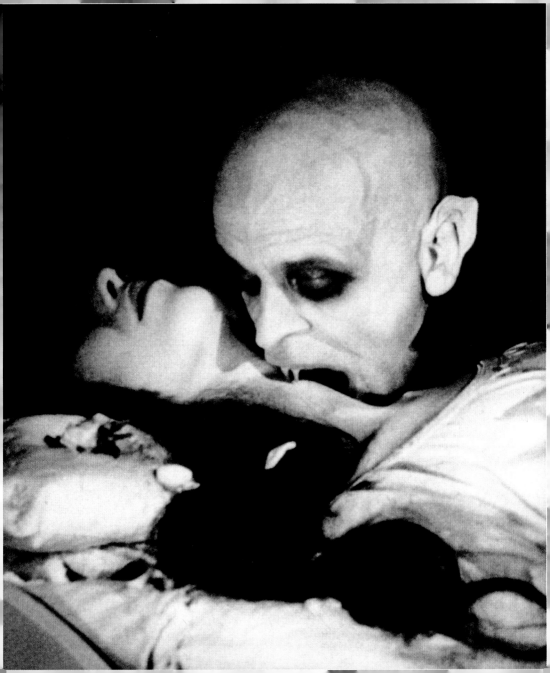

WHERE TO BITE

A vampire can bite anywhere he chooses on the body. Indeed, one of the easiest areas to feed from is the wrist, which is usually fairly slim and easy to get the teeth into, so it is often the site vampires choose to feed an initiate the blood that will turn them into a vampire. The other location, of course, is the chest or breast, as employed by Dracula when seducing Mina. However, the area traditionally most usually chosen as the place for the bite is the neck (regardless of how awkward it is to actually get a grip on it with fangs), or the junction of neck and shoulder, which is a little easier to manage.

A sensitive spot

The choice of the neck is quite understandable: it's a relatively easily accessible sensitive zone as well as containing one of the more important arteries and veins: the carotid, which carries blood to the brain, and the jugular, which carries it back for reoxygenation. Both of these are alarmingly close to the surface of the skin in comparison to other veins and arteries, adding a shivery thrill of danger to any bite.

The nature of the bite

The bite itself can be hurried and savage, leaving a badly bleeding, life-threatening gash, or more restrained and less damaging, resulting in two neat puncture wounds and some bruising. In some traditions the incision is made with the vampire's long, sharp nail instead of his fangs, resulting in a cut rather than a puncture. The vampires using this method don't have fangs and can therefore pass as human much more easily.

Bite to Kill

 Some people believe that the vampire is nothing but pure evil and will always kill his victim, justifying the death as necessary in order to hang on to his anonymity and secrecy— although the random discovery of dead bodies drained of blood is likely to be anything but secret.

Another school of thought suggests that the victim is killed so that there is no risk of their soul being damned by their rising as an undead creature. This, though, would demonstrate compassion and religious faith on the part of the vampire; rather at odds with the fact that they are nevertheless killing a human. Neither theory is satisfactory, although both seem to say that creating an undead takes a conscious act on the part of the vampire.

PICKING A FIGHT

Science fiction and horror magazines became very popular after World War II. This *Weird Tales* jacket, from July 1949, shows two demons fighting. The artwork was by Matthew Fox.

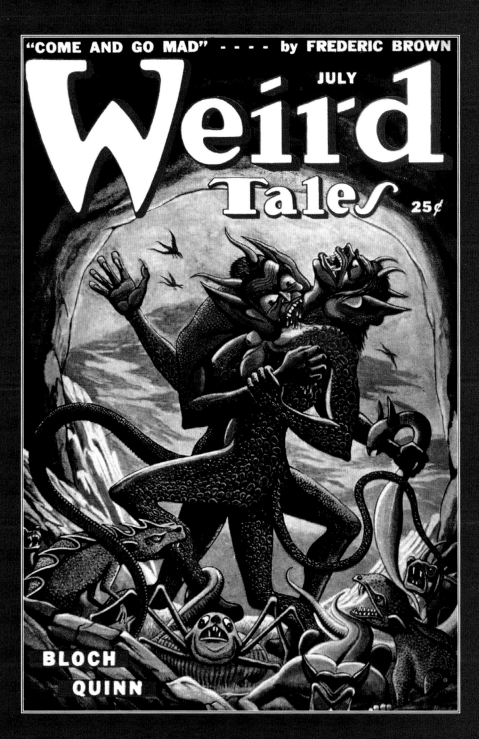

Why "Turn" a Human?

There are three main reasons why a vampire should want to "turn" a human.

THE NEED FOR COMPANY

The first is for companionship, to have someone like himself to share adventures, experiences, and interests. Being a vampire is a lonely existence: human friends and family age and die; fashions and customs change; and politics, technology, and the very pace of life shifts swiftly when you can live forever.

All the benefits

Being a vampire is exciting to start with, but as the years, decades, and then, finally, the centuries slowly pass by, the realization that you can never go back, that the past is lost and all that is left is a lonely and uncertain future, the desire for a companion can become overwhelming. If this is the case the vampire may not let on about the details of a vampire's former life. He may emphasize, instead, all the benefits involved in being able to live forever, experiencing the progress of civilization as it hurtles on through the millennia.

A SPECIAL SOMEONE

Secondly, the vampire may turn a human because he wants someone to control, someone to serve and worship him, no matter how reluctant they are. Having power over another can be addictive, especially if the vampire was weak or helpless in his mortal life. In such a situation the "master" simply won't consider his victim's feelings, choosing someone who takes his fancy and who he will probably see as expendable. The master will certainly not reveal everything he needs to know about survival as a vampire to his disciple, as a way of making sure that he doesn't stray.

TURN FOR LOVE

Thirdly, "turning" may be done out of love, or to save a loved one from an untimely death. This is usually the most difficult decision to take, as well as being the most difficult to justify. If you love someone, do you really want to condemn them to undeath? Even if by not doing so you doom them to an early grave?

Making the decision

The responsible vampire will agonize over the decision, and may resist even suggesting it to the other until they are forced by circumstance, or by the other requesting it. This is usually the case with the noble vampire Saint-Germain (see page 39), who takes his responsibilities very seriously and makes sure he tells his partner everything before allowing them their wish. Even then he warns them again of the disadvantages.

An overlap

Of course there is quite likely to be an overlap between all the different reasons for becoming a vampire. For the sophisticated vampire, love

Vampirism as Mutation

 We've come a long way from the days when it was believed that an evil vampire spirit possessed the empty shell of a mortal, moving in, taking up residence, and animating the dead flesh.

Now it seems more likely that vampirism is a form of mutation, or a virus or disease passed to the human through the blood or saliva, which forces the body to reshape itself permanently. This is why the transformation is painful: having your organs twisted and distorted to allow for your new life isn't going to be comfortable.

The film *Twilight* refers to the venom that the vampires pass to their intended initiates through their bites. *Interview with the Vampire* speaks about the pain as the initiate's body "voids its human wastes" and the pain of the sudden realization that the newly turned vampire will never see another dawn (in that particular tradition, anyway, where the sunlight is lethal to vampires).

without companionship, or companionship without at least a little love, would be impossible. And, as shown by Lestat de Lioncourt and Louis de Pointe du Lac in the *Vampire Chronicles,* lust and the dual desires for a friend as well as someone to dominate can create an interesting dynamic. The relationship between Bella Swan and Edward Cullen, in the *Twilight* series, is based primarily on love and a desire to protect the loved one.

THE TRANSFORMATION

Once "turned," the victim will become a fully fledged vampire. This can take place either immediately or up to a month or so later, although the period of three days seems to be the most usual.

The process

As the change happens, the victim's human body dies and reforms as vampiric, unable to digest anything but blood. It is stronger and more durable than a mortal body, and its senses are enhanced. In most cases the victim remains conscious during the transformation and usually suffers, since it can be extremely painful.

Survival techniques

The initiating vampire, often called the "master," usually teaches the new vampire how to survive; what situations and people to avoid—all the small, important aspects of vampire life. This teaching may come before transformation, especially if the reason for the initiation is love or companionship, so that the human knows what to expect.

The Habits of Vampires

Nobody seems to quite agree on how vampire society is structured. In some traditions the solitary vampire is almost violently territorial, killing any other vampire that trespasses onto his patch, but there are other far more sociable possibilities.

UNITS AND PACKS

Some vampires may live and travel in a small family-type unit, with two or three members, like Louis, Lestat, and Claudia in *Interview with the Vampire*. In others, such as in the *Twilight* and *Underworld* movies, the vampires form what could almost be called a family, living relatively peacefully in a mutually supportive group.

Group protection

In yet other situations, such as the book *Kitty and the Midnight Hour*, the vampires have formed a pack, or perhaps a flock would be a better term, for their own protection, and have clearly defined territories that they defend, although discreetly and diplomatically, from the neighboring werewolf pack.

Pros and cons

There are pluses and minuses in both ways of living. There is often safety in numbers, as the Parisian vampires believed in *Interview with the Vampire*, but with all the group together, one dedicated vampire hunter can destroy a whole community before they even awake, let alone take any action. A vampire alone may be able to hide more easily and can move more quickly, but it is vulnerable to attack, especially if there's more than one hunter.

FEEDING HABITS

Vampires generally don't feed from other vampires and why this is is far from clear. One school of thought states that once the blood enters the vampire's body it loses its nutrient value and combines with whatever it is in undead blood that can pass the condition onto humans, and is therefore "dead" for another vampire.

Too tempting

Another idea is that it's because vampire blood is too delicious for other vampires, tempting them to drain the one from whom they're feeding, making it a dangerous activity.

Yet another theory states that it's the trust and love of the donor that makes the drinking of blood so important for the vampire. In that sort of feeding, the vampire takes in the life-energy the blood contains, and this would be impossible with another vampire.

Blood addicts

Whatever the cause, though, the ultimate sin for a vampire is to kill another of his kind, because it's a thrill quite unlike any other and can become dangerously addictive.

A CLOSE FAMILY

In the 1999 film *The Little Vampire*, vampires form a close-knit family group. Human boy Tony wants a friend to add adventure to his life and what he gets is Rudolph, a vampire kid with an excellent appetite. The two become inseparable friends.

Vampire Lifestyle

SAFE HAVENS

Whether it's a castle, a penthouse, a mausoleum, a crypt, a cave, or a hole in the ground, the vampire must have a safe place to return to during the sunlight hours, and the refuges he chooses vary widely. However, a vampire caught at sunrise will have to find the nearest, darkest, most light-proof place he can, even if that is a sewer. One thing that all vampires must bear in mind, however, is that no matter where they live, they will never show any signs of aging, and somebody, eventually, will notice.

Moving on

Different vampires deal with such matters in different ways. Saint-Germain, the Cullen family, Henry Fitzroy, and Nick Knight, the vampires who have most contact with the human world, accept that they must move on whenever people become too observant and curious. The world is large, and there are always ways of earning a living that will allow interaction without danger. Big institutions always need night workers, low-key individuals who will do the least-liked jobs. On the other hand, some vampires have developed the trick of returning as their own son or cousin, making provision in their wills for such an eventuality.

Other vampires simply move to a new country and don't return until a generation or a century has passed. Of course, all this becomes harder in a world where everything is documented and proof of identity is needed for even the simplest activity. It may, eventually, be necessary for vampires to make their existence known and become part of human society.

ACCUMULATING WEALTH

With care, a vampire can live for thousands of years, quite possibly forever, if he doesn't grow weary of life and opt to end it, or have it ended for him. He can certainly live long enough to acquire vast riches. Money or goods stolen from early victims paid into a high-interest account or trust fund by a friendly human can increase dramatically over the years. The rise and fall of stocks and shares is less risky when you have centuries to play with, and in the computer age daylight trading is no longer required, although it might make it a little more difficult to maintain the anonymity needed for survival. There's always a way around such problems: there are plenty of hackers looking for a challenge.

A STILL FROM DRACULA

A still from the 1992 horror-romance movie *Dracula*, starring Gary Oldman as Count Dracula. Based on the original book by Bram Stoker, this film version made a few controversial changes to the original story, which some people objected to.

Vampires & Their Humans

Most supernatural beings tend to be solitary individuals. Let's consider some of the others that might cross our paths. Ghosts are insubstantial, unable to feed or touch; werewolves are mostly human except for full-moon nights, although the more modern ones are able to change voluntarily (and some much prefer their fur-form); zombies are mindless unless they are controlled; and ghouls shun humans, in the main.

The vampire, however, for all his strengths, is vulnerable to humans, and to human interference during his daily sleep, when he is easy to stick a stake into or to burn.

BEING IN THRALL

There may be considerable overlap in the ways that vampires create a thrall (see page 182), depending on the individual. Thralls generally do whatever their master demands. This can range from offering their own blood as nourishment to kidnapping victims to feed his bloodlust, to running interference for him, even sacrificing themselves so that he can escape.

A Special Relationship

Some vampires have thralls. These are humans who serve a Vampire Master. Thralls can be created in several ways:

➜ *The vampire can drink from humans, and in some cases allow the human to drink in return, creating a psychic, mental, or telepathic bond, but this is not a true vampire. It may be necessary to stake such a human after death to prevent them from rising again as a member of the undead.*

➜ *The vampire can hypnotize the human into serving him, although that can be self-defeating as the thrall may need to be given detailed orders if his will or mind is damaged.*

➜ *The vampire can seduce the human into obeying him. The sheer ecstasy that being seduced by a vampire can provide may act like a drug, transforming the human into a willing and devoted slave.*

➜ *In some cases, usually where a noble vampire is involved, there is no compulsion: the human simply loves and respects the vampire so much that they are happy to serve for no more reward than friendship.*

➜ *The vampire may hold the human's family hostage to obtain their obedience.*

What Vampires Regret

Sunrise has been a symbol of hope since humans first started to mark the passing of time. Sunrise meant that the dark had not won; that eyes adapted to daylight would be able to spot predators and enemies, providing the opportunity to fight or run to safety. It meant that warmth would return to the world. It's unsurprising that the Sun was first seen as a goddess, spreading her bounty over the Earth.

GIVING UP DAYLIGHT

Becoming a vampire has mostly meant giving up the daylight world. Two famous vampires particularly regret the fact: Louis of Anne Rice's *Vampire Chronicles* and Nick Knight of the *Nick Knight* film and the *Forever Knight* television series. Both have, however, found a way to alleviate that lack by watching the Sun at second-hand. Louis enjoyed sunrises at the cinema, watching as the celluloid art moved from jerky black and white, through films of the real thing, to computer-generated views of sunrise from space. Nick dealt with the problem slightly differently—by having cameras on the roof of his home feed down to the TV screens inside.

MISSING FOOD

Some vampires miss ordinary, human food. The youngsters in *Vampire High* spend a few minutes reminiscing about what they had for their last meal as mortals, and it's very clear that they would dearly love to be able to eat real food still.

But with the transformation comes an inability to digest solid nourishment—for most traditional vampires anyway.

MAKING UP

Many vampires, especially as they age, deeply regret the lives they have taken in their fight to survive. They may attempt to make up for things by devoting their time, money, and knowledge toward making the world a better place for all.

Losing everyone

Most of all, vampires may regret the fact that they will lose everyone they know, everyone they love, unless they condemn those people to the same fate as themselves. To be a vampire is to submit to a life of loneliness.

As Josie says, "Being human means being mortal. It means dying. You can't rob people of that. You're offering something you have no right to... Never a birth? Never a death? That's not evolution, that's a full stop."

Being Human, Episode Five

The Vampire's World

There are advantages to being a vampire, of course. Immortality is a precious gift, if you know what to do with it. Imagine being able to follow what's happening in the world of technology right through the ages; to see the age-old scourges of disease brought under control and finally defeated; to be there when the first colonists set foot on their new world.

Delaying aging

It may one day be possible for humans to delay, or even defeat, the aging process, creating immortal humans who might even become friends with their vampire kin.

AN ENHANCED WORLD

How does the world appear to a vampire? The descriptions we have are wonderfully evocative. Every sense is enhanced: colors are deeper and more vivid, and there are more of them, as the vampire eye can see further into the electro-magnetic spectrum than the human eye.

Lifting the veil

Karl, in *A Taste of Blood Wine*, describes this change like having a gray veil lifted from his eyes, letting him see properly for the first time; even his own skin seems to glow like an opal. Louis, in *Interview with the Vampire*, says it was as though he had never seen shapes and colors before, and the moonlight on the flagstones had him so entranced he must have stared at it for an hour.

There is an intensity of color, of light and shade, that can't be seen by human eyes. In practical terms, such eyesight is of great advantage to a predator, but it also helps esthetically to make up for the loss of the colors of daylight.

BLOODSHOT EYES

The eyes of old vampires are often shown badly bloodshot or even completely red, a trend often followed in the early vampire movies. Most modern vampires, with their greater need to blend in with human society, are depicted with compelling eyes, large and dark with a hypnotic quality, although the eyes of the vampires in the *Underworld* films become almost iridescently pale when their powers come to the fore.

Most recently, however, movie and TV vampires have possessed eyes that, no matter what their normal color, turn completely black when the hunger strikes, or when they are hunting. It can be argued that this is actually the iris enlarging to fill up more of the eye, of great advantage to a predator, as it enhances night vision.

HEIGHTENED SOUND

Sound is also hugely enhanced, both quality and quantity. The vampire can hear the human pulse, the blood racing through veins, and count the number of people in the area by the number of heartbeats. They can tell if a building is inhabited, and by what, by the sound of the heartrate.

Vampire Reproduction

 The thorniest question about vampires, however, is whether the undead can have babies. It seems most likely that the vampire can't reproduce like a human—though there are even exceptions to that. The vourdaki of the *Haadri Cycle* reproduce like humans, but are exceptionally fertile, the females conceiving every time they make love. They cannot, however, interbreed with their humanoid cousins. In Elaine Bergstrom's series of books about the Austra family, *Shattered Glass*, *Blood Rites*, *Blood Alone*, and *Nocturne*, the family are hereditary vampires and able to have children, although the ability does come at a cost to the women. The babies aren't exactly what humans would consider normal, of course. The vampires in *Fever Dream* can also reproduce, although since the babies claw their way out of their mother's womb very few female vampires ever volunteer.

SUPERIOR SMELL

The sense of smell is superior, too, and that again is helpful for a predator, especially since it's cued into the scent of blood. This can, however, cause significant problems for the hungry vampire surrounded by warm, blood-pulsing, blood-fragrant humanity.

THE SENSE OF TASTE

Taste—well, with such a limited diet the sense of taste is less important, although the vampire seems able to appreciate the tastes of different blood types (see page 114) and skins.

Different flavors

It's been suggested that the human's diet flavors their blood, especially strongly flavored foods such as garlic and onion—although the average vampire might prefer to avoid such people— and certainly in *Interview with the Vampire* Lestat seems to enjoy feeding from humans who have had an alcoholic drink or two, as he is able to feel the warmth and intoxication of mild inebriation at second hand.

The influence of drugs

It may be that drugs, especially hallucinogenic drugs, also have something of the same effect on the vampire as on the human physiology, although it could be argued, given that the vampire's existence is perilous enough at the best of times, he might prefer to avoid such individuals. The loss of control involved when the human ingests such narcotics may loosen his own control, and that could well turn out to be deadly for a vampire.

The vampire's sense of touch is more sensitive than a human's, as well. It's no wonder the modern vampire has the reputation of being such a superlative lover, when he feels so inclined, being able to smell and taste the emotions of the body beside him, to cultivate passion, and respond to every tiny nuance of feeling.

VAMPIRE STRENGTH

The supernatural strength of the vampire depends on which tradition is preferred. All vampires are stronger than humans, but it varies between only a little stronger, enough to be able to fight off an attacker or carry one's coffin around, to being strong enough to make a crime scene look as though a tornado ripped through it.

Additional strength can make for a much easier life, but it can also spark human curiosity: generally speaking, it's wisest for the vampire to pretend to be only as strong as a human of comparable size and build.

In *True Blood*, although they can make love, the vampires can't sire children or conceive them. It's as though his ability to reproduce by "turning" humans takes over from his physical attributes: the only penetration he is now capable of is his fangs in the soft flesh of his lover or victim.

HYPNOTIC CHARM

The hypnotic charm and telepathy some vampires use often come from the same source and is quite obviously tied to the fact that the vampire is a predator. It's much easier to feed if you can charm prey into a complete lack of resistance.

Hypnotizing animals

Interestingly, some vampires seem to be able to hypnotize animals as well as humans—which is probably just as well when feeding from a large animal. Trying to drink with a horse or cow noisily and violently objecting to being bitten is going to be at least a little painful, regardless of the strength and invulnerability of the vampire. Invulnerable does not mean impervious to pain.

Hypnotic effect on humans

This particular skill comes into its own when dealing with humans, of course. It takes a particularly strong-willed individual—or an absolutely terrified one—to resist the vampire's subtle, erotic, seductive control. And given the vampire's looks, and the flattery of his attention, the prey is usually predisposed to give in. Fortunately, being a supernatural creature, the

---

Vampire Speed

A vampire's speed is also far superior to humans', and may explain why they can seem to appear suddenly without anyone seeing their progress, although the ability to move absolutely silently helps, and is an adaptation of great use when hunting. As with strength, the speed at which each vampire can move varies greatly.

The Rhode Island Vampire

In the last two decades of the 19th century, the Brown family of Exeter, Rhode Island, was plagued by tuberculosis. The horrible, incurable at the time, and usually fatal disease could kill slowly and torturously, over years, or it could be quick, taking only a few weeks. It attacked the lungs, leaving the victim short of breath and very weak. The skin turned pallid and gray, the sufferer lost weight, and skin could draw away from their teeth and nails, making them look more like claws and fangs. They frequently coughed up blood as well. In fact, they could look like both a vampire and a vampire's victim!

In the case of the Brown family, the mother, Mary was the first to die in 1883, followed seven months later by the eldest daughter, also called Mary. The only son, Edwin, contracted the disease two years later and was sent to live in Colorado, in the vain hope that the dry air would help. In 1891 he came home to die: in the meantime his sister Mercy also contracted the disease and died soon afterward.

Friends and neighbors suspected that the family's problems were being caused by a vampire, and the bodies were exhumed. The two Marys' bodies had decomposed, but Mercy seemed freshly interred, and when her body was cut open, liquid blood was present in her heart and liver. Her heart was cut out and burned, and the ashes mixed with water and given to Edwin to drink, naturally this was to no avail. The poor young man died a couple of months later.

It's generally agreed that Mercy wasn't a vampire: she had died in the winter and her body stored in a crypt until the ground had unfrozen enough for her to be buried, which effectively meant she'd spent the time since her death in a primitive freezer, which preserved her body. However, the event caused widespread interest at the time, and supports the idea that a vampire can be the scapegoat for any natural illness that can befall a living human. At least in this case the suspect was already dead...

vampire is generally invulnerable to harm and unlikely to be infected with the nasty ailments that plague humans, remaining untouched by malaria, HIV, guineaworms, or lice!

Being thick-skinned

This is probably also true in the case of bodily harm. It's been suggested that some vampires' skin is resistant to damage—in the case of Meyer's vampires the skin is so hard apparently very little

can hurt it—but we've also seen it can be cut, and in mortals anything that can be injured like that can allow infection to take hold. But this just doesn't appear to apply to vampires. Though, of course, their ability to heal extraordinarily quickly also helps.

HEALING ENERGY

It takes energy to heal, though, energy gained from feeding, and the worse the injury the more energy that is needed. If a vampire can feed soon after being having been injured, and then take some rest, he is normally just about fully healed by the time he wakes. However, if he's not able to feed, it can take much longer.

SUSPENDED ANIMATION

What happens if a vampire can't feed for a prolonged period of time? He may, if he's lucky, go into a kind of suspended animation to wait until it's safe to feed again. He may start to age, possibly, if forced to go without blood for long enough, even until he reaches the age he would be if he were alive—and how terrible it would be to be trapped in that sort of withered husk!

Worst of all, though, and the sort of punishment vampires mete out to others of their species who have broken their commandments or endangered the flock, is to be sealed in his coffin and left to starve—the terrible fate Louis was condemned to by the Parisian vampires in *Interview with the Vampire* to pay him back for the way he dealt with Lestat.

Recovery and revival

A feed of fresh, hot blood after a prolonged period without feeding will revive a vampire, but it may take a good many such feedings before he is fully recovered. And if he can't escape, if he is trapped in a sealed coffin with no way out, what then?

A TRUE DEATH

If the vampire is immortal, he will starve, slowly and surely, but he will not die. There may eventually be nothing left of him but a skin-wrapped skeleton, but life will remain, dimly fluttering deep in sunken eyes. Although by this time the vampire will, most likely, be insane. The kindest thing to do may well be to let him burn in sunlight, to experience what Saint-Germain calls "the True Death."

Less able to cope

Immortality may, ultimately, prove hollow. Over and above the loss of everyone the vampire knew, everything familiar and comforting, he will find himself growing less and less able to understand and cope with the demands of a more and more technologically based, faster world. He is, to some extent, frozen in time, a lonely icon of his own culture and age.

Immortality

Humans may long for immortality, but in the end it removes the compulsion to strive, to achieve, to make life better, to give birth to the future. All that's left is a being with no drive or desire, one who can only react to events, not shape them.

A STILL FROM DRACULA

A shot from *Dracula*, starring Gary Oldman. Gazing into a goblet of the blood he needs to sustain him, he is reminded of the frailty of life and the loss of his beloved Elisabeta.

Do Vampires Have Souls?

"For the blood is the life."

Deuteronomy 12:23

BLOOD AND RELIGIOUS PRACTICE

Blood has always been an essential part of religious practice. We see it in Abraham offering up his son, Isaac, as a blood sacrifice to Yahweh, and the Druids stabbing the sacrificial victim in the belly and divining the future from the agonized twitching of his body and the patterns of his blood.

The Mayans sacrificed their people to ensure that the Sun rose the next day; and the priest raises the cup of wine aloft for it to become the blood of Christ given for the redemption of sins. Since humans first conceived the idea of gods the offering of blood to a deity of choice has stained the history of the human race with crimson.

Parallels

There are some obvious parallels between religious beliefs and the lore of vampirism. At Catholic mass and Anglican communion the priest offers us the blood of the crucified Christ to remind his people of his sacrifice for their sins, as Jesus commanded the disciples to do in remembrance of him at the Last Supper. The vampire's willing victim offers up their blood, but more significantly, the vampire's offering of blood to his prey imparts the gift of eternal life—just as the blood of Christ is said to do.

Rebirth

The vampire in many traditions rises from death to a kind of new life in three days, which is what Jesus was said to have done at the Resurrection.

The modern vampire, like Jesus, has shed his mortal flaws and is reborn in a new and beautiful body, strong and lacking all the ailments, frailties, and weaknesses of the old one. But where Christ has, they say, ascended to Heaven, the vampire is Earthbound, alive to enjoy and share his immortality where he desires.

Baptism?

We could even argue that for the victim to drink the vampire's blood is a form of baptism, aimed at bringing the human over into the vampire's world much as religious baptism welcomes the believer into the family of the Church.

Historically the Church calls the vampire evil, blasphemous, and an abomination, but there is no proof of the religious vision of an eternal afterlife, while the vampire is proof that he can bestow earthly immortality on his chosen.

Importance of the soul

One of the tenets of Christianity—of most religions, in fact—is the belief in the soul; that insubstantial, unprovable but important part of every human being which makes them what they are. It's the part of us that survives the death of the body, and, the Church would have us believe, goes to Heaven or Hell after death. But does a vampire have a soul? If he does, then he can be "saved": if he repents God will forgive him and accept him into Heaven. But if he has no soul, is he truly a damned creature, destined to return to Hell to dwell with his master the Devil once he's set free from his earthly existence?

Reanimated corpses

It was easier in the old days: it was believed that a vampire was a corpse reanimated after death by a demon. His soul had moved on to wherever it was destined to go, and that was the end of it. Destroying the shell that was left was a matter of good sense, ensuring he couldn't pass on his contagion to anyone else. These days, however, we don't believe in demons...

SEDUCTIVE EVIL

What the Church calls "evil" in this case is seductive. The vampire promises excitement, decadence, even danger. He takes us out of our boring daily life and makes us someone special, just for a little while.

The vampire fulfils the role of tempter beautifully. In a world becoming increasingly secular, and turning away from the restrictions of faith as a civilization demands physical proof and an explanation for everything, the allure of such a supernatural creature is very strong.

Top Ten Male Vampires

This is a list of the top ten most well-known male vampires in movies and literature.

⇥ *Dracula*, the original Master Vampire, complex and compelling: resurrected over and over again in numerous books and films.

⇥ *The Comte de Saint-Germain*, the most ancient vampire of all: noble, compassionate, and wise.

⇥ *Henry Fitzroy*, royal bastard (in both senses of the words): strong, fast, and charismatic.

⇥ *Mitchell*, the tortured soul trying desperately to be human.

⇥ *Don Simon Xavier Christian Morado de la Cadena-Ysidro*, old, world-weary, and ruthless.

⇥ *Lestat de Lioncourt*, amoral adventurer through life.

⇥ *Viktor the Elder*, powerful and absolutely without mercy: divorced from humanity, his strange mind is difficult to understand for mere mortals.

⇥ *Edward Cullen*, lonely and lovelorn.

⇥ *Angel*, the vampire who knows what it's like to exist, both with and without a soul.

⇥ *Barnabas Collins*, the tragic vampire, doomed to survive in a world without the one thing that made his life worth living—his wife-to-be.

The Science Of Vampires

There are a number of medical conditions that may have contributed to the vampire legend.

RARE DISEASES AND DISORDERS

"Porphyria" is term referring to a group of at least seven rare hereditary diseases. They are due to a reduced ability of the sufferer's body to produce heme, a molecule in red blood cells that is essential for transporting the oxygen that the body needs to survive. The diseases fall roughly into two types: acute (hepatic) porphyria, which affects the nervous system and causes abdominal pain, vomiting, seizures, hallucinations, depression, and paranoia, and cutaneous (erythropoietic) porphyria, which makes the skin sensitive to sunlight, shrinks the skin of the gums and lips, and increases hair growth. The condition can be managed, but there is no cure.

People suffering from cutaneous porphyria are very pale, and the shrinking of skin in and around the mouth makes their teeth stick out more. Both types of porphyria can also turn the urine purple, which may be mistaken for blood by those who don't know and be the source of one of the legends about the vampire gorging himself on blood so much that he excretes it instead of urine.

Skin ailments

There are three skin ailments that may be mistaken for vampirism. Polymorphous light eruption (PLE) causes hypersensitivity to sunlight.

Exposure, sometimes even just a few minutes of winter sunshine through a window, causes an intensely itchy rash of blisters, which can take up to two weeks to clear.

More serious is actinic prurigo. While the symptoms resemble PLE, they last all year and can cause blistering of the lips and conjunctivitis. The most serious is xeroderma pigmentosum; a rare but tragic hereditary skin condition causing extreme sensitivity to ultraviolet light and premature skin aging. Even a brief exposure causes sunburn; longer exposure causes cancer. Sufferers must avoid the Sun completely, and often die under twenty years of age.

Sensitivity to light

Light sensitivity, where the eyes become unusually sensitive to even moderate light levels, can have a number of causes, but the result is often painful and debilitating, requiring special glasses and avoidance of bright lights, especially sunlight. Sufferers flinch away from sudden bright lights and cover their eyes, actions that may suggest vampirism to the gullible.

Anemia

This is a common disorder in which the body can't transport oxygen effectively. It can be caused by a lack of iron in the body, excessive blood loss, blood cell destruction, or inefficient blood-cell production. Sufferers may appear extremely pale,

The Vampire of Croglin Grange

Croglin Grange in Cumbria, North-West England, it is said, belonged to the Fisher family for centuries, until in the early 19th century they moved into a larger home. The Grange was put up for letting, and eventually, after a long hard winter, the Cranswells, two brothers and their sister, rented the place.

One summer evening, as she prepared for bed, Miss Cranswell happened to glance out of the window toward the adjoining graveyard, and saw, to her startlement, what appeared to be a pair of glowing red eyes moving above the headstones. Disturbed, she locked her bedroom and tried to sleep.

On the point of nodding off, she was brought abruptly awake by rustling outside the window. Sitting up, she saw the demonic eyes and hands scrabbling at the window: they pried off the lead from two of the triangular glass panes, pushed them out onto the floor, then one hand reached in to open the latch.

Too terrified to scream, Miss Cranswell watched the tall, shadowy, cadaverous figure of a man climb in, and moments later her brothers were awoken by her frantic screams. Smashing down the door, they found her bleeding to death from gashes on her neck: too busy trying to save her life, they couldn't spare the time to follow the figure that flitted back to the graveyard.

After a recuperative spell in Switzerland, Miss Cranswell volunteered to act as bait while her brothers tried to catch the foul creature. In a repeat of the first attack the figure gained entry to her bedroom, but her brothers lay in wait and both fired their guns. Hit, the creature fled the Grange and raced back to the graveyard.

The next day the brothers, accompanied by the servants, tracked the creature to the graveyard, where they found an open crypt. Inside were broken coffins, their contents scattered and gnawed, but in one corner stood an untouched casket. Inside they found the body of the night's attacker, apparently dead, its eyes cold and glassy, but there was a bleeding pistol wound in its leg. They dragged the creature out into the sunlight, and burned it to ash. No-one ever discovered the identity of the supposed vampire, nor why it waited to attack until the Cranswells had moved into the Grange.

weak, short of breath, and weary—all signs, to the unenlightened, of a victim of vampire attack who is about to become a vampire themselves.

Sleep paralysis

This condition occurs in that brief period when we are either dropping off to sleep or just waking up, when our brain and body aren't quite operating in sync. We can see and hear and think, but not move, as the body is still in that state of paralysis that is part of REM sleep. This paralysis is perfectly natural and automatic, and stops us acting out our dreams, thus keeping us safe. Sleepwalkers are lacking in the function.

Unable to move, we may feel as though there is something evil just out of view, and a weight pressing down on us, preventing us from breathing—all symptoms of a "vampiric attack," and all perfectly natural, if terrifying at the time.

Premature burial

The nervous condition catalepsy may have been the cause of premature burials in the past, before human pathology and physiology was properly understood. The body becomes rigid, the breathing and heartrate slow, and the person fails to respond to stimuli, including pain.

To the untrained eye the sufferer may seem dead, even though they may be able to see and hear what's happening. It's easy to imagine the terror of the sufferer "waking up" in a coffin. It's equally easy to imagine the reaction of mourners at the funeral to the screams coming from inside that coffin. And if the unfortunate didn't wake up in time, clawmarks on the inside of the coffin where they had tried desperately to escape, would only have fueled the vampire myth.

BLOOD MEMORY

Bill Nighy as vampire Viktor the Elder in *Underworld: Rise of the Lycans*, a 2009 movie. In the Underworld films, blood carries memories, and any vampire who drinks it will have the full memory of the person, vampire, or werewolf to whom it belonged.

Psychology of the Vampire

FREUD AND VAMPIRES

For Sigmund Freud, the founder of psychoanalysis, the fascination with vampirism comes from a perfectly human interest in, and fear of, illness and death, combined with suppressed sexuality and aggression. Freud also saw vampirism as an externalization of "the unconscious Oedipus complex" that he believed all children experienced and needed to work through in order to become healthy individuals. The correlation between blood drinking and suckling milk from the mother, both of which provide sustenance, lends some credibility to this idea.

JUNG'S BELIEFS

Carl Jung, the psychologist, however, saw the vampire as an expression of the Shadow, that archetype that expresses the instinctive, amoral side of the human psyche.

Lestat as the Shadow

Lestat (see page 39) from Anne Rice's *The Vampire Chronicles* is the most exuberant example of the Shadow: he revels in his amorality, and we are outraged and secretly jealous of him for it. The vampire allows us to project all our own nastiness into an external, supernatural figure, thus permitting us to learn to deal with it. For some people, this may act as a useful release of pressure. For others it can go too far. Letting the Shadow take over is not a wise thing to do.

Pathological narcissism is, essentially, a need to be admired, given meaning from an outside audience. The sufferer chooses to construct a grandiose version of his own reality, performing for others as though on a stage, living the fiction he has created for himself.

He needs to be in control and to be seen to be in control. The figure of the vampire, a larger-than-life creature, is ideal for his purposes and may be adopted as his persona.

Renfield Syndrome

Traditionally known as "clinical vampirism," Renfield Syndrome is characterized by an obsession with drinking blood. The name comes from the Count's servant (in *Dracula*) who ended up in Seward's asylum working his way up from eating flies to birds in his obsession to become like his master.

Originating in a traumatic event in childhood that makes the sufferer find blood or drinking it exciting, the condition has four stages. The original incident is the first, followed by the urge to drink one's own blood, then to drink the blood of animals, and finally the blood of other humans.

The person believes that blood has life-enhancing powers, giving the drinker control over the victim, which is certainly true if he resorts to murder to feed his compulsion.

Notorious "Vampires" of the Past

 Countess Elizabeth Báthory (1560–1614) known as the "Blood Countess," was a Hungarian noblewoman who used her position to lure young women to their deaths.

Peter Kürten (1883–1931), dubbed the "Vampire of Düsseldorf," may have suffered from a form of Renfield Syndrome. Born into extreme poverty, Kürten's early life was blighted by his violent, abusive, and alcoholic father. The family of 11 children lived in one room. Kürten was a self-obsessed psychopath, and completely unable to empathize with anyone else. On his arrest in 1930 he confessed to 79 offences.

Fritz Haarmann (1879–1925), the "Vampire of Hanover," lured his victims to his apartment, where he would kill them by biting through their necks. He murdered at least 24 men in this way, dumping their remains into the river.

Joseph Vacher (1869–1898) of France, murdered at least 11 people, sucking their blood as they died.

In the late 1870s **Vincenzo Verzenia** of Italy murdered two individuals in order to drink their blood.

Neville Heath (1917–1946) of England, murdered, mutilated, and drank the blood of two women.

Andrei Chikatilo (1936–1994) of Russia, dubbed the "Red Ripper," was only able to satisfy himself through violence and blood. He was eventually convicted of the abduction, mutilation, and murder of 52 women and children.

Richard Trenton Chase (1950–1980) killed and mutilated six people, including a baby, because he believed he had to drink blood to replenish his own, which was being turned to powder by Nazis.

Marcello de Andrade was guilty of the murder of 14 young boys in Rio de Janeiro in 1991. He believed that drinking young blood would keep him young and beautiful.

In 2002 **Allan Menzies** of Scotland, murdered Thomas McKendrick in order to drink his blood: he believed that Akasha, the "Mother" vampire in *Queen of the Damned*, was speaking to him telepathically, telling him what to do.

Human Living Vampires

Human Living Vampires, HLVs for short, are individuals who believe that they are a separate species from humanity, sharing some of the characteristics of their mythical counterparts. There are two sorts: the sanguinarians, who drink blood, and the psychic vampires, who feed from the life energy (*ka* or *chi*) of others.

SANGUINARIANS

Sanguinarians have a psychological need to drink human blood, and many believe that they possess some unusual qualities, such as enhanced vision (especially at night), unusual sensitivity to sunlight, and the ability to sense other "vampires." Some also claim enhanced strength and stamina and increased resistance to disease, though none claim to be immortal or undead. In reality, none of these have been proven to be true, and while the human body can digest blood, as anyone who enjoys rare steak can attest, large amounts (anything over a pint, generally speaking) are more likely to cause vomiting than anything else. Most of the blood is excreted like any bodily waste. The HLVs compulsion to drink

A Real Vampire?

In 1918 a Mrs Hughes had taken up residence in a small house at Pennlee, Strete, near Dartmouth in the South West of England: this area is legendary for hauntings, UFO sightings, and a wide variety of strange and supernatural happenings. On this occasion, the housekeeper came downstairs to find a muddy footprint in the middle of the polished wooden floor. To everyone's alarm it was clearly in the shape of a cloven hoof.

The house was small, as were the closed windows: there was no way an animal could have entered. Nevertheless they searched the building carefully, but found no other disturbance.

Over the next few nights, Mrs Hughes found herself being physically attacked by an invisible being. It left her so frightened that in the end she resorted to hanging garlic all around the house. This stopped the attacks and peace returned to the building.

Famous vampire hunter, Montague Summers, in *The Vampire in Europe*, speculated that perhaps the vampire in question was old or weak and so unable to fully materialize and take its sustenance in the usual way— otherwise the results might have been very unpleasant indeed.

From Ken Taylor's book *Dartmouth Ghosts and Mysteries*

blood serves no useful physical purposes—anemia is more readily treated by eating iron-rich vegetables or taking iron supplements if necessary—and can be extremely dangerous due to the number of currently incurable diseases and viruses that can be transferred through blood: HIV and hepatitis are probably the most worrying.

Suitable protection

To protect themselves, sensible sanguinarians will insist on potential donors being tested for disease before accepting them as a source of blood, but much of the time blood donation and drinking is a matter of trust between the people involved. In any event, it's rare for the sanguinarian to actually bite the donor.

Wrong design

Human teeth aren't designed to pierce the skin, and even with custom-made fangs, the human mouth is the wrong shape to make a neat bite. It is also full of extremely dangerous bacteria (human bites should always be given urgent medical attention). Instead, incisions are made with sterile blades and are usually fairly small, and often made by the sanguinarian's donor: the amount of blood taken is a matter of personal choice or "need."

PSYCHIC VAMPIRES

Conscious psychic vampires are another matter entirely. Most tend to be responsible creatures, and try to control their abilities so as not to be a literal drain on others. Such beings could be confused with succubi, although they are different from the true, demonic succubus (see page 183). Others may find that the abundant life energy to be found in Nature is more than sufficient for their needs. Anyone who finds that a hike in a forest or in the hills leaves them feeling energized and refreshed, rather than tired, may be a psychic vampire of this sort.

EMOTIONAL VAMPIRES

Emotional vampires can be dangerous. If they feed on negative emotions—anger, jealousy, hate, misery—they may do all in their power to generate these emotions in their victims while giving nothing back. This can make for a very miserable life indeed.

Anyone who has ever been in a self-destructive relationship with such a person will know how wretched and depressed, even suicidal, that can make the victim feel. The only way out is to break off, though by the time it has become a real problem that might be very difficult to do. Outside help and counseling is often required.

Whether being a HLV of any kind is a choice or a medical or psychological condition isn't clear, and is beyond the scope of this book. What it does serve to do, however, is make the HLV feel special, different, unique; a need we all have.

Defences Against Vampires

There are almost as many defences against the vampire as there are vampire myths.

EVERYONE AT RISK
In days gone by there were a number of ways to prevent susceptible people from becoming vampires in the first place. Just about everyone was at risk of becoming one!

If the vampire managed to survive, it could rise from the grave, usually after three days, in imitation of the three days between Christ's crucifixion and resurrection, and begin to prey on the living. To stop it, the body could be exhumed and exorcized, or staked, decapitated, and burnt. Where it was believed that sunlight destroyed the vampire, dragging it out of its coffin and leaving it to burn in the Sun was also an option. Fire is the one element against which flesh, human or vampiric, has no defence. It purifies, but in so doing it destroys utterly.

VAMPIRE AT LARGE?
How did one tell if a vampire was on the loose? It usually attacked its immediate family first, drinking their blood and making them pale and ill, though it could also attack the family's animals. If that didn't slake its thirst, it would turn

---

Those Most at Risk
In various European countries those at risk of becoming vampires included:

→ *Those born with a caul (the face or head partly covered by the amniotic sac that protected the baby in the womb), teeth, or a tail.*

→ *Those who had been conceived or born on certain holy days.*

→ *Those who had been excommunicated.*

→ *Those who had been the subject of incorrect burial rites.*

→ *Babies who died before being baptized.*

→ *Witches and sorcerers.*

→ *Heretics.*

→ *Anyone who had led a sinful life.*

→ *Anyone who had eaten an animal killed by a vampire.*

→ *Anyone whose corpse had been jumped over by an animal, especially a cat, prior to burial.*

→ *The victims of a vampire.*

→ *Those who had committed suicide.*

to neighbors and friends, gradually enlarging its pool of victims. Sometimes it would take whole villages this way. It acted like the Plague, and was sometimes used as a scapegoat for the deaths caused by that relentless disease.

Finding the culprit

Exhuming recent corpses, or the bodies of those upon whom suspicion fell, and inspecting their contents was the only way to find the culprit.

Any body that hadn't decomposed, seemed fresh or had blood on its lips, or that seemed younger since drinking blood, was thought to reverse the aging process for a vampire, was to be decapitated and the heart taken out and burned. The ashes were then mixed with water or wine and drunk by those who had suffered the vampire's attacks: this would cure them of the weakness and disease inflicted by the undead. And if it didn't cure the victim? Well, there were always other recent graves that might hold the vampire.

It's unknown how many graves were desecrated thanks to this malign superstition. It may be safe to assume that it was a large number.

DETERRENTS

Vampire deterrents were many and varied, and often the same as for other supernatural creatures as well as witches. Hawthorn is supposedly particularly lethal to supernatural beings, and the stakes for staking vampires should be made of the wood. A branch of hawthorn over the door of a house repelled evil of all kinds. A branch of wild rose in the coffin might also pin the vampire in its grave. Iron implements were supposed to be proof against all kinds of evil, too, and an iron stake was as effective as a wooden one for dispatching a vampire. Silver wasn't only for werewolves: in some traditions it was effective

Precautions

To prevent individuals from rising from the dead to trouble the living, the family should:

→ *Remove and burn the caul from the baby, in the hope it would not become a vampire after its (hopefully much later) death.*

→ *Bury a body facing downward, so that the vampire could only dig down toward the earth rather than upward to its prey.*

→ *Pin a body in its coffin with stakes through the flesh and into the ground below the coffin, so that it couldn't move.*

→ *Place a cross or crucifix in the coffin.*

→ *Decapitate the corpse and separate the head from the body. In some traditions placing it between the feet ensured that the body could not rise.*

against vampires as well. A silver bullet in the heart would stop either creature.

Making bread with the blood of a vampire mixed into the flour was also thought to prevent the creature from attacking those who ate it, whether they had yet been targeted or not.

The power of mirrors

Mirrors were anathema to the undead. The vampire, lacking a soul, cast no reflection: upon being reminded of the fact he would shriek and lash out at the mirror, smashing it to pieces. In later lore, this lack of reflection in mirrors has been extended to include tapes and film, making it impossible to record a vampire on any audio or visual medium.

Religious icons

Since vampires were evil, religious icons, such as crosses, crucifixes, holy water, and the Eucharist wafer, if a priest could be persuaded to part with one, would naturally keep them away.

Garlic

Garlic was also a powerful deterrent, and the juice was often rubbed around window and door frames and keyholes to keep safe all those within. Garlic was pretty much a universal cure-all before the days of standardized medicine. It has antibiotic and antifungal properties, and has been used for centuries to alleviate colds and many other ailments: the fact that it is such a good, useful plant, in combination with the strong smell as much as the pungent oil, was believed to repel all manner of evil.

The power of counting

Another rather strange belief was that the vampire was obsessed with counting. Scattering mustard seed on the ground, or in some lore sawdust, grains of wheat, or sand, would force the vampire to stop in order to count the seeds or woodflakes, and be unable to move on until he'd numbered every last one.

This delaying tactic could allow his prey to escape, or keep him occupied while hunters found and dealt with him. Some authorities recommended putting the seed or grain in the coffin itself, as a way of keeping the vampire inside, as he would still be forced to count them, and even with his enhanced vision counting in the pitch darkness wouldn't be easy.

Native soil

A long-standing belief is that the vampire must rest on his native soil in order to maintain his existence. By removing the soil from his coffin, or placing a religious icon, such as a cross, upon it while he was out hunting, meant that he couldn't

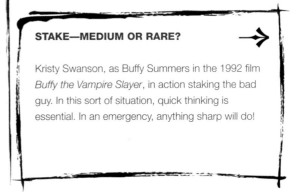

STAKE—MEDIUM OR RARE?

Kristy Swanson, as Buffy Summers in the 1992 film *Buffy the Vampire Slayer*, in action staking the bad guy. In this sort of situation, quick thinking is essential. In an emergency, anything sharp will do!

get in on his return, and could force him either to be burned to final death by the light of the rising sun or go to ground elsewhere. This second option only applied if he was in his own country, of course, but given that he usually returned to his grave with only a little time to spare, finding another resting place, or digging one, would have to be done in a great hurry. There would usually be signs of disturbance that vampire hunters could use to determine where he had hidden.

Entering a building

Traditionally, a vampire was not able to enter a building unless he was invited in by someone who actually lived there. The thinking behind this has changed in modern times so as to allow a vampire to enter a publicly owned building, such as a library, hospital, or office, without being invited, since such places aren't actually dwelling places.

MODERN TECHNOLOGY

As religious beliefs and the power of the Church faded and science advanced inexorably, the old weapons, the crosses, and holy water often had

no effect. These days the battle is more often fought with modern technology, though the trusty stake and heavy knife or sword are always good to have in case of unforeseen emergencies.

Nasty!

Ultraviolet light is one of the main weapons, either as torches to scorch the vampire's external form or as "bullets" that will burn the creature up from inside—a nasty touch seen in the *Underworld* movies.

Although silver is the primary weapon against werewolves, the purity of the metal has led to some authorities stating that it is also effective against vampires. This in turn has led to the use of silver nitrate-filled bullets being employed as an effective high-tech weapon.

HORROR OF DRACULA

Christopher Lee stars as Count Dracula in *Horror of Dracula*, the 1958 movie. In this still he is shown cringing before a crucifix, so that he is forced into a position in which he is exposed to the harmful rays of the sun; the only way he can be destroyed.

Vampire Hunters & Slayers

There is a certain amount of cross-over between "vampire hunters" and "vampire slayers" (see page 48), however, "hunter" suggests a human that happens to have expertise, while "slayer" implies some degree of extra physical abilities. Here is a list of the most well known:

→ **Abraham Van Helsing** Dracula *(books and movies).*

→ **Anita Blake** Anita Blake: Vampire Hunter *novels.*

→ **Buffy Summers** Buffy the Vampire Slayer *(movie, TV series and spin-off books).*

→ **Blade** Blade *(comics and movies.) Blade is a dhampir (see page 71).*

→ **Michael Colefield** Ultraviolet *(TV series).*

→ **Carlisle Cullen** Twilight *Carlisle hunted vampires with his father before becoming one himself.*

→ **D** Vampire Hunter D *(Anime and books).*

→ **Edgar and Allan Frog** The Lost Boys *(movie).*

→ **Gabriel Van Helsing** Van Helsing *(movie).*

→ **Harry Keogh** The Necroscope *(novels).*

→ **Magiere and Leesil** The Noble Dead *series of novels. Magiere is a dhampir, Leesil a half-elf.*

→ **Sean Manchester** *Self-styled vampire hunter and author of* The Highgate Vampire.

→ **Javier Mendoza** Blood Ties *(TV series).*

→ **Robert Neville** I Am Legend *(book and movies).*

→ **Peter Vincent** Fright Night 1 and 2 *(movies).*

→ **Zero Kiryu** Vampire Knight *(Anime).*

"Our very existence is a union of life and death. Cemeteries, hospitals, funeral parlours are all places where the two worlds meet and overlap. We feel at home here. These are our churches."

Herrick, *Being Human*, Episode Five

UNDERWORLD: EVOLUTION

Kate Beckinsale stars as Selene in the Len Wiseman directed horror thriller *Underworld: Evolution*. Named for the goddess of the Moon, Selene is a Death Dealer, a vampire who is dedicated to the total wiping out of werewolves.

The Vampire-Hunter's Toolkit

 In the world of fantasy and make believe, no self-respecting vampire hunter is seen dead, or undead, without a toolkit, much as a serving soldier would feel undressed without a gun. After all, a vampire hunter never knows when they might run into a member of the vampire fraternity...

First and foremost, a vampire hunter would always carry a mirror. The vast majority of vampires cast no reflection so the mirror is used to confirm an initial diagnosis.

Stakes are also absolutely essential. Whatever kind of vampire they come up against, a stake through the heart will mark its end. Of course, a stake through the heart will also kill a human, so it's very important for the hunter to be a hundred per cent certain that the adversary is a vampire before action is taken.

Wooden stakes are the cheapest and easiest to come by: so recycled wood or branches from a dead or dying tree are important if the hunter is into DIY. Silver or iron stakes are a lot more expensive, especially if they are to be left in the vampire to make sure that he cannot escape.

To complement the stake, a hammer of some kind is required: unless the hunter is supernaturally strong he or she will have some difficulty doing the deed. The actual size of the hammer is a matter of personal choice and may partly depend on how much the hunter wants to carry around: if the hunter is naturally strong a smaller hammer will do.

It's always useful if the hunter includes a bottle of holy water and several crucifixes. Not all vampires will react to the religious icons, but it's better to be safe than sorry.

A large, heavy knife is a useful implement, especially if decapitation of the undead becomes necessary. A whetstone or some method of sharpening the knife is a good idea.

A small container of mustard seed or sand might be handy, to keep prey distracted during attack or escape.

Lastly, a few cloves of garlic are a must. If they don't help to keep the vampires away, they can always be used in a bolognaise sauce later.

WARNING: While the information given above is accurate, it is meant to be read in a humorous manner. We DO NOT recommend taking action against any putative vampires, and carrying dangerous weapons, with or without intent to use them, is both unethical and dangerous to both the self and others, and may be illegal. When in doubt, check with a professional.

THE TOOLKIT'S CONTENTS

This splendid toolkit, the pride and joy of a dedicated vampire hunter, contains a whole range of crucifixes, some ornate and others plain, plus a couple of sturdy stakes and a robust-looking hammer.

Chapter 2

The Origins of Vampires

Blood is the Life

It's not so surprising that the human imagination created a creature that drank blood. From the first time a human made the connection that too much "red stuff" coming out of a body made it pale and weak, and losing a little more made the person dead, blood has had a magical, mystical power. It represents life itself. Drinking blood is drinking life, and drinking another person's life gives the vampire a connection to its victim, along with power over them.

THE NATURAL HISTORY OF THE UNNATURAL VAMPIRE

The vampire has existed in the myths, legends, and folklore of almost every nation and at almost every time. From the tragic *langsuyar* of Malaysia to the malicious *fifollet* of Lousiana and Voudon, via, of course, the European *vampyr:* the undead have always been with us.

The beginning

But where did the idea of the vampire come from? To answer, it helps if we imagine life before anyone knew about the human body, when the only medical treatments usually involved herbal trial and error or blood-sucking leeches. But everyone knew about life and death; it was all around them, all the time. And they knew what the priests told them about what happened when their lives ended: their soul either went to Heaven or to Hell. What they didn't know was that sometimes the boundary between life and death wasn't quite as clear-cut as they believed, and that there were some medical conditions, like narcolepsy, that could imitate death.

The spirit world

The widespread fear of spirits and demons was often a carry-over from primitive times and primitive religions, and they could be blamed for anything and everything that couldn't be explained. Crops failed? A demon had withered the plants. Sick children or animals? They were being attacked by demons. Unable to have children? Well, obviously your woman was being cursed by a demon. Child born deformed? It must have been a demon's child...

The rising dead

In this world of fear and helplessness it would be very easy to believe that the dead could rise again. After all, the Savior did. But everyone knew that the soul passed on after death, so what was putting life into the body? Must be a demon.

No doubt there are other explanations for the belief in vampires, but because of the traditional nature of the undead, this is as valid as any. Humans have always peopled their world with spirits; even these days with our technology and knowledge and when we could be close to discovering the origins of the Universe. Fear and ignorance breed superstition, and humanity is always looking for ways to combat the darkness.

Where Vampires Live

THE WORLD'S EARLIEST VAMPIRE

Perhaps the earliest recorded vampire was the *edimmu* of Mesopotamia. Dating from more than 6,000 years ago, this furious, violent victim of a burial that hadn't been done properly not only drank the blood of passersby but could suck them dry of life energy as well, making them the first known "psychic vampires."

Wreaking havoc

Although their anger was directed mainly toward those who had not followed funeral rites correctly, the *edimmu* also preyed on more or less anything that was still alive. They caused disease and family disasters and inspired criminal activities in otherwise law-abiding people who had not actually known the malevolent creature when it was alive. Their wrath was terrible, bringing all kinds of bad things and death to their victims and destroying whole households.

These days, it is said, the *edimmu* hide among the homeless in big cities, bringing with them a life of disease and misery and living among derelict buildings. A fitting home, perhaps, for a revenant whose final resting place was a ruined, desolate, unvisited grave. Related to the *edimmu* was the blood-sucking *akhkharu*.

Meanwhile Babylonian demonology talks about the *lilu*, a vampiric fiend who preyed on newborn babies and pregnant women. One of them, the storm demon Lilitu, who brought death to those she touched, was later adopted by the Jews as Lilith, the supposed first wife of Adam (see also page 116).

The ancient Roman *strix* was a night demon that often took the shape of a screech-owl, flying after dark to drink the blood of small children. Its Greek counterpart was the *lamia*, although she was shaped like a serpent rather than a bird, and seductively beautiful. Also Greek were the *keres*, red-clad haunters of battlefields with terrifyingly sharp claws, gnashing teeth, and a ferocious appetite for blood.

The *bruxsa* of Portugal was a female vampire who seduced and tortured lonely travelers, returning to suck her own children's blood; a thoroughly nasty creature who frightened anyone who was setting out on a journey.

Bringing corpses to life

The old Sanskrit folklore of India tells of the *vetala*, a spirit that lived in corpses, causing them to reanimate: it slept just like a bat, hanging upside down from the trees in cemeteries. Its close cousin, the blood-drinking *rakshasa*, was a shape-shifter as well as a blood-drinker, hunting prey in the form of a large bird. Lower down on the undead scale was the *pisacha*, who was stupid, violent, and ugly, and haunted graveyards and ruins.

Another vampiric Indian being was the *churel*. This sad creature was created from a woman who died in pregnancy or while giving birth, or while having her period. She always sucked the blood of young men, draining them of their life until they aged much faster than they should and died.

VAMPIRES OF AFRICA

In spite of its variety of complex and ancient mythologies that are still around today, Africa had, according to Montague Summers, only two vampiric creatures: the *asasabonsam* ("monstrous creature") and the *obayifo* ("witch vampire"). The first looked human, except for its iron teeth and hook-shaped feet, which it used to catch its victims from a perch in a tree, hauling them up into the branches to drink their blood. Since it lived deep in the forest it was rarely seen and not considered much of a problem.

A ball of light

The *obayifo* was a different matter. As a witch living anonymously within a community, it was impossible to tell who might be an *obayifo* and who was not—although shifty eyes and a reluctance to meet people's gaze were possible signs. In some accounts these creatures had the power to leave their bodies and travel to their victims as a ball of light; in others they kept their human form, except for shining a phosphorescent green light from the anus and armpits, both of which, you'd have thought, would make them easy to spot. In both cases they drank the blood of their victims, mainly children, causing them to die from a slow and painful death. The penalty for being an *obayifo* was death by burning.

Firefly shape

However, more African vampires have come to light since Summers was writing. The Ewe people of Ghana speak of the *adze*, a blood-sucking creature that takes the shape of a firefly and can pass through closed doors in its hunt for victims. It was particularly feared because there was no way of defending oneself from it.

The *impundulu* of southern Africa has an insatiable thirst for blood. It usually takes the shape of a large bird and can create thunder with its wings. It may also take the form of a handsome young man in order to charm and feed from female victims.

SOUTH AMERICAN REGIONS

There are similar vampiric creatures throughout the Caribbean. The *loogaroo* (a corruption of "loup garou," French for werewolf) of Grenada and Haiti usually takes the daytime form of an old woman who has a pact with the Devil, bringing him hot, fresh blood in return for evil powers.

A VAMPIRE SERPENT

Polish surrealist Biegas Boleslas painted the vampire as a monstrous femme fatale. This 1914 oil on canvas image appears to be inspired by the Greek serpent vampire, the Lamia.

DEMON WARRIOR

Particularly evil humans might be reincarnated as *rakshasa* after their death. These blood-drinking, man-eating demons were shape-shifters and illusionists: they desecrated graves, hounded priests, and could even possess humans.

PREYING ON THE VULNERABLE

Vampire bats about to attack a woman blissfully asleep in a hammock. This engraving was done in South America in 1882. When European explorers found these nocturnal bloodsuckers, they were quickly absorbed into contemporary stories, with some vampires taking the form of bats.

Shedding skin

The *sukuyan* of Trinidad is an old woman who sheds her skin at night, while the South American country of Surinam has the *asema*, a blood-sucking sorcerer that appears as an old person during the day, but at night hunts its victims in the form of a ball of blue light.

Belief in these, along with the *fifollet* (feufollet) located in the Louisiana swamps, was probably brought over from Africa with the slaves, and gradually became mixed into the native myths.

Death bats

In Mayan mythology, the cave-dwelling god Camazotz, which was human in form, but possessing the head and wings of a bat, may have been inspired by *desmodus draculae*, the giant vampire bat that was native to Brazil, Guatemala, and Mexico.

He was closely associated with fire, death, night, and sacrifice and, of course, blood. Belief in "death bats" was widespread until at least 1976, and may still continue right up to the present day.

THE GHASTLY CHUPACABRA

The *chupacabra* is said to inhabit parts of the Americas, but is especially associated with Puerto Rico, Mexico, and the United States, especially in Latin American communities. The name translates as "goat-sucker," from its habit of attacking livestock and drinking the blood.

Shape-shifter

The *tlahuelpuchi* of Mexico is a particularly nasty form of vampire. Born cursed with the shape-shifter condition, he is protected and hidden by his family, out of fear more than love, as anyone who kills him will be afflicted with the same curse.

His powers become apparent at puberty: he is a shape-shifter, taking on the form of animals such as dogs, cats, or buzzards to hunt, and he has to feed between once and four times a month on blood or he will die.

The blood of babies

He will feed at other times, of course, though not necessarily every night. His much-preferred food is the blood of babies who are less than a year old, although he will take adults if he must.

He can operate during the day if absolutely necessary, but his favorite time is between midnight and just before dawn: he can get into locked houses by shape-shifting into the form of an ant or flea.

Continuing belief

The *tlahuelpuchi* are territorial and aggressive toward their own kind. Onions, garlic, and metal objects can be used to repel them and may be used to keep the creature away. Belief in the *tlahuelpuchi* carries on, even up to the present day. It is said that the last known execution of a female *tlahuelpuchi* occurred in 1973.

The Mexican vampire, *civatateo*, was a servant of the Aztec Tezcatlipoca, the god of discord, deceit, and sorcery. A high-caste woman who died in childbirth, she fed on young children and had a taste for young men: the offspring resulting from these affairs would always be vampires.

The goat-sucker

More recent is the legend of the *chupacabra*, the "goat-sucker" of Mexico and Chile, so called because it only attacks livestock. While this version is not a humanoid vampire, it's worth noting because people still say they see it today.

The *chupacabra* is described as being either a reptile-like gray or greenish creature that hops like a kangaroo, or a kind of strange, hairless wild dog with a ridged spine. It drains the blood of its prey completely.

Feeding habits

And, of course, there's always the vampire bat of South America. They were first noticed by Europeans in the 16th century and their common name comes from the similarity of their feeding habit to the ancient legendary vampires of the Old World and not the other way around.

There are three species of vampire, Common, Hairy-Legged, and White-Winged. All three exist solely by consuming blood and their saliva contains a substance, draculin, which prevents their prey's blood from clotting while they feed. They can be extremely dangerous to both humans and animals, as they can pass on blood-borne diseases such as rabies.

VAMPIRES OF GREAT BRITAIN

UK folklore talks of several vampiric beings. The *baobhan sidhe* (pronounced baa'van shee) was the part-elven vampire of the wilds of Scotland.

The dance of death

Appearing as an irresistibly beautiful woman, *baobhan sidhe* entranced and seduced her victims, inviting them to dance with her until they were eventually exhausted. She then drained them of their blood, piercing the flesh with her long fingernails, which became talons when she was ready to feed. Her usual prey was young men or hunters, the latter probably more frequent victims as the *baobhan sidhe* lived in the forests and hills, shunning inhabited areas. She could be warded off by iron and sunlight would kill her.

Seducing young men

The *lhiannan shee* is the Manx counterpart of the *baobhan sidhe*. A malevolent vampire, she took the form of a beautiful woman in order to attract and charm young men, drinking their blood and sapping their life-force by degrees until they eventually faded and died. Her beauty was an inspiration to poets, for whom she could be a muse, and whose premature deaths were blamed on her powers. It's important not to confuse her with the Irish *leanan sidhe*, who, although still supernatural, symbolized intelligence and creativity, and inspired the young artists who took her as a lover. Although not evil, her lovers suffered and longed for her when she wasn't there because their artistic abilities were enhanced. Her beauty was often seen as dangerous.

A vampire to tame

One of the more tragic vampires originates in Malaysia. The *langsuyar* can be beautiful, a lovely and charming woman with long, luxuriant hair and unusually long, sharp nails.

The legend says that the first *langsuyar* was a noblewoman. On hearing the news of the death of her recently born child, she died of shock and became a vampiric demon, afterward feasting on the blood of infants through a hole in the back of her neck.

A woman dying in childbirth or immediately afterward may also become a *langsuyar*. Legend says that, rather like the *selkie* of Scotland, the *langsuyar* can be "tamed." Cutting her nails and hair and stuffing the cuttings into the hole in her neck forces her to take on a human form, at least until the cuttings fall out and she goes back to her *langsuyar* form and vanishes.

The pontianak

Even more heart-rending, the stillborn or recently dead child of the *langsuyar* usually becomes a vampire itself—a *pontianak*. It lurks in the forest, crying piteously, as though abandoned or lost, only to attack the person who rescues it. It then sucks the victim's blood as it would have sucked its mother's milk.

VAMPIRES IN CHINA

The Chinese vampire, the vicious *kiang-shi* or *chiang-shih*, possessed several of the limitations that some traditional European vampires suffered. They were very pale, with heavily defined dark circles around their eyes, were nocturnal, and had great difficulty in crossing water.

However, they drank *qi,* or life energy, rather than blood—although that didn't stop them ripping the heads off their victims. They traveled by hopping, since moving their legs was intensely painful once rigor mortis set in.

Violent death

Kiang-shi were believed to be created after a particularly violent death, by suicide, hanging, drowning, or smothering. The soul clung to the body, keeping it animated even though the flesh was actually dead. *Kiang-shi* were very difficult to kill, but a human could avoid being attacked by holding their breath: *kiang-shi* were supposedly blind and tracked their prey by listening for their breathing.

VAMPIRES DOWN UNDER

Even Australia had its own Aboriginal vampire, the *yara-ma-tha-who*, a small, red, man-shaped creature who lived in large trees. It had no teeth, but the ends of its toes and fingers were shaped like octopus suckers, and it drank the blood of people who had fallen asleep under the tree.

Building up an appetite

When the sleeper was so weak that he couldn't escape, the *yara-ma-tha-who* would take a nap or go for a walk in order to build up an appetite. On returning to its prey, it would drop to the ground and crawl to its victim, then swallow him whole like an anaconda.

That was not the end of it, however. The *yara-ma-tha-who* would, after a little while, vomit its victim back up, still whole and usually alive. The creature would then poke, tickle, or jump on its victim to see if it was still alive.

Pretending to be dead

If the victim could pretend to be dead for long enough, until the *yara-ma-tha-who* needed to sleep, they stood a good chance of being able to escape, because the *yara-ma-tha-who* was only able to waddle slowly.

If they couldn't escape, however, the creature would swallow them again, and regurgitate them later, repeating the actions over and over again, with the victim shrinking in size each time. Eventually the victim would become a *yara-ma-tha-who* himself.

Western Vampires

Many of the best-known vampire lore comes from the Slavic cultures of Central and Eastern Europe and the Balkans from around 500 CE onward. The term "vampire" comes from the Serbian, although the root of the word is uncertain—it may be related to "witch" or "to fly."

GO MAD FOR VAMPIRES

What can only be called vampire hysteria swept through Europe in the 17th and 18th centuries. Every nation had its own version of the creature, many of them with the same features, weaknesses and methods of destruction as each other.

Frightening and bloodthirsty

Bulgarian vampires, or *obours*, were bold and destructive, terrifying villagers with their howling and shrieking, while the Hungarian *oupire* drained the blood of humans and farm animals with equal enthusiasm.

The Polish *upior* and *vjesci* (pronounced "vyeskee"), and the Russian *upyr* all consumed vast quantities of blood from both people and animals, stole the hearts of their victims, and floated in blood-filled coffins when they slept.

Power over the elements

In Romania the *varcolac* and *moroi* preyed on the living, hunting sometimes in the shape of a wolf or a cat, drinking the blood and eating the hearts of their relatives. The *nosferatu* of Transylvania and nearby regions, as well as drinking blood, could cause men to become impotent, and hold power over certain elements, such as rain, wind, and fog. This was a common feature of many vampires of the area. They were altogether quite a charming bunch!

SURGE IN INTEREST

However, in the late 18th century there was a resurgence of interest in the fantastical, the gruesome, the supernatural, and the occult. This was partly a backlash against the grim, hard, mechanical culture that had been created by the Industrial Revolution. It seems that humans needed to find a balance in a world that was focused on harsh reality.

Sophisticate

Then, in 1819 John Polidori introduced the world to the first fictional vampire sophisticate, Lord Ruthven, in his short story *The Vampyre*, and the world has never looked back. The work was originally published as the work of the already-famous writer Lord Byron.

In fact, Polidori was Byron's friend and physician, but both men knew that the name of "mad, bad, and dangerous to know" Lord Byron would help the story's fame. The suggestion that the character of Lord Ruthven was based on Lord Byron added to the writer's antihero image and to the idea of the vampire as both a nobleman and seducer.

The Dhampir

 The dhampir is a rare and intriguing creature; a hybrid, half-human, half-vampire. It's rare because a vampire, being essentially a reanimated corpse, is unable to reproduce in the same way as a human.

However, in some traditions it can take several days for a vampire's victim to die and rise as a vampire himself, and in these cases, if he can make a human woman pregnant, the child may be born as a dhampir.

Alternatively, if a pregnant woman is "turned" by a vampire when she is close to having a baby, the result may also be a dhampir: this method is the origin of the dhampir known as Blade, of the comics and *Blade* films.

Dhampirs have all the positive abilities that vampires have; speed, strength, enhanced senses, ruthlessness, and the ability to heal quickly, but none of the disadvantages, except for a need for blood, and even this may only surface when the dhampir is stressed or angry.

They usually become vampire hunters, and are generally very successful since they can tackle vampires at their own level. They have no problem with sunlight, the vampire's greatest weakness, which gives them additional power.

The dhampir is driven by hatred and the need for revenge against the creatures who took from him the mortal life that should have been his birthright and who violated his mother before he was born.

For some, the need for blood is an ever-present temptation to give in to his base vampiric urges and attack those he is dedicated to protecting. It makes him very dangerous and unpredictable, both to humans and to vampires.

Dhampirs' weapons include the traditional sword (for decapitating the vampire), a gun (with wooden bullets or ultraviolet flares), hawthorn to trap the vampire in its resting place, or wooden stakes for staking.

One particular type of dhampir hunter, the *djadadjii*, "bottled" vampires, luring them into a bottle half-full of blood, before sealing them in and then throwing the bottle into a fire.

Well-known Dhampirs

The most renowned dhampirs are:

→ *Magiere, the heroine of the* Noble Dead *books by Barb and J.C. Hendee.*

→ *D, the hero of Hideyuki Kikuchi's* Vampire Hunter D *books.*

→ *Vampire Princess Miyu, of the Anime and Manga of the same name.*

→ *Alucard, the hero of the* Castlevania *computer games.*

→ *Alek Knight, anti-hero of Karen Koehler's* Slayer *series.*

→ *Possibly* **Mina Harker** *in* The League of Extraordinary Gentlemen, *although hers is a slightly different case (see page 111).*

BLADE II →

A still from *Blade II*. The dhampir Blade, played by Wesley Snipes, is immensely strong and completely ruthless, sparing neither vampire nor human thrall in his dedication to wipe out the undead threat.

Vampire Theories

Here are some of the many theories about how the very first vampire came into being:

Lilith and Adam

The first wife of Adam, Lilith, flew away on his refusal to agree to their being equal. Adam went to God, saying that she had run away (but not why). God sent three angels to bring her back, with the threat that if she did not agree to be subservient to Adam a hundred of her children would die every day. Lilith, the original feminist, refused, and from then on was cursed to become a blood-drinking, child-murdering demon.

Akasha

In Anne Rice's *Vampire Chronicles*, Akasha, a queen of Ancient Egypt, is a shallow, self-obsessed creature. Becoming fascinated with the supernatural, she has the witch sisters, Maharet and Mekare, brought to court to summon spirits, from which she then demands the answers to trivial questions. One particularly bloodthirsty spirit, Amel, attacks her and enters her body as she is on the point of death after being assassinated. Amel fuses with her own spirit and creates a new entity; immortal, unable to bear the light of the Sun, and thirsting for blood. Akasha thus becomes the "mother" of all vampires, first passing the "gift" to her consort, Enkil, and then to others. Over time the two become immensely strong and less and less human, eventually turning into living statues, called "Those Who Must Be Kept"; kept safe and hidden, that is, as they are the source of vampire existence. If they die, all vampires die.

The corvinus strain

In the *Underworld* movies, Alexander Corvinus survives the Great Plague, but it mutates his DNA, making him immortal. He goes on to have two sons, Marcus and William, both carrying the DNA: William is bitten by a wolf and becomes the original werewolf, while Marcus is bitten by a bat and becomes the original vampire.

Vourdaki

The vampiric *vourdaki*, in the *Haadri Cycle*, are mutated offshoots of the humanoid heartlings. The two distinctly different and discrete species separated somewhere between fifteen and twenty thousand years ago.

Marvel comics

In the Marvel Universe, the fictional continuum in which the stories in the Marvel comics take place, the first vampire was an Atlantean sorcerer called Varnae who was turned into a vampire by the followers of a powerful necromancer using the Darkhold—the Book of Sins, a grimoire of black magic. The vampire's first act was to consume one of those who had created him. He went into hibernation when Atlantis sank, to reappear millennia later as and when the writers needed an ultimate vampire villain.

The Highgate Vampire

In the late 1960s reports of a strange figure haunting the venerable and beautiful Highgate Cemetery, in London, led to an unfortunate spate of vandalism from would-be occultists.

Two local men, David Farrant and Sean Manchester, became interested in the matter, and Manchester, a self-styled vampire-hunter, who claimed to be the descendent of an illegitimate son of Lord Byron, determined to rid the world of what he declared was a vampire, an unnamed European nobleman who had been buried on the site before the cemetery was built there.

There was no evidence to support the claim, although both told the press that they had seen foxes drained of blood and sporting throat wounds. Manchester declared his intention to hold a vampire hunt on Friday 13 March 1970. It became a much publicized local event, with major TV coverage and hordes of "ghost-hunters" from all over London converged on the cemetery, breaking in despite police attempts to keep them out and causing considerable damage.

Manchester claimed that he and his associates gained entry to the cemetery and found the suspect crypt, but the coffins were empty, so all they could do was sprinkle holy water and place garlic inside. Some years later, Manchester claimed to have found, staked, and burned a vampire in the Highgate area, possibly implying that it was the same undead. There does not appear to have ever been any evidence to verify the event, however.

The Crystal Ring

One of the most startling and original depictions of the world from which the vampires originate is in Freda Warrington's vampire trilogy, *A Taste of Blood Wine, A Dance in Blood Velvet,* and *The Dark Blood of Poppies.* There exists a place, or a feature, or perhaps a phase of existence, they call the Crystal Ring, which, like the atmosphere that envelops the physical world, surrounds a shadowy aspect of the world that only immortals can enter. It's a hostile, alien place. Here everything is distorted and twisted into impossible shapes and colors: the sky seems to flow with liquid light and fire, and the Earth's lines of magnetic force shimmer like the aurora. Charlotte, the original human main character, believes the realm's structure to be created by the electrical energy generated by the thoughts of billions of human minds, by their dreams and emotions. Karl, her vampire lover, isn't so sure.

Kristian, the probably-insane, manipulative despot of the realm, believes it to be the mind of God, and vampires, his ruthless dark angels. Whatever you believe it to be, it is both terrifying and horrifically beautiful, ever-shifting, ever-changing. To stay there for any length of time is to go mad.

The Vampire & Archeology

 Bodies decompose and wooden stakes rot: finding archaeological evidence of vampires isn't as easy as you'd think. However, there have been several recent cases of the graves of suspected vampires being discovered.

The oldest of these is at an early Bronze Age burial site in Mikulovice in the Czech Republic. Among all the normal four-thousand-year-old graves is one in which a man has been laid to rest with a heavy stone placed on his chest and another on his head—a precaution taken, it would seem, to stop the vampire from rising from his grave to prey on the living!

In 1966 at Celakovice, just outside Prague, a 10th- and 11th-century cemetery was found to have a number of graves where apparently anti-vampire rituals had been performed on the bodies. In some a nail had been driven into the head; in others heavy weights has been placed on the body; and in yet others the head had been cut off and turned to face downward, so that the undead couldn't find its way out of its grave to haunt mortals.

In 1990 the Walton Cemetery, Griswold, Connecticut, was discovered under a sand and gravel business site. Among the graves of about 30 people who died between 1750 and 1830 was the resting place of one man, identified as J.B. by the tacks on the lid of the coffin. Inside there was clear evidence that the body had been exhumed and tampered with: the thighbones had been removed from their rightful place, and with the skull, placed at the head of the skeleton in a skull and crossbones arrangement.

A local newspaper account of 1854 makes it fairly clear that the residents believed in vampires: they'd dug up and burned the bodies of two brothers they'd suspected of being undead and preying on the living. It's been suggested that in the case of J.B., the body was too decomposed to allow the heart to be cut out and burned, which was the usual cure for vampirism, so instead the family detached the head and legs so that the vampire would not be able to rise.

In 2006 a grave was found in Venice, Italy, with the skeleton of a woman inside—with a brick between her jaws. Local people apparently did this to suspect corpses so that the vampire could not bite anyone!

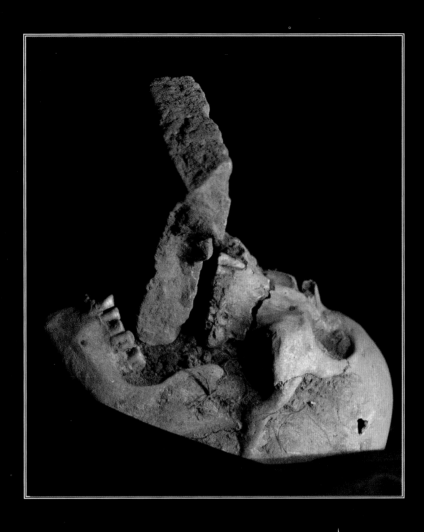

A BRICK BETWEEN THE TEETH

This is the 16th-century remains of a woman with a brick between her jaws unearthed in 2006 in an archaeological dig near Venice, northern Italy. Experts say this is evidence that she was believed to be a vampire. The unusual burial is thought to be the result of an ancient vampire-slaying ritual.

Chapter 3

The Evolution of Vampires

Vampire Development

"For centuries the vampire has had to feed on humans to survive, hunted by day, hunting by night, but as times change and history evolves, so must the vampire."

Introduction, *Sundown: the Vampire in Retreat*

Before Stoker's *Dracula* took the reading world by the throat, several other vampire stories had already been published, giving dire warnings to the public that such creatures moved among them. *Carmilla* was one; the "penny dreadful" *Varney the Vampire* (see opposite) another, but the story that started it all was *The Vampyre* by John Polidori. Published in 1819, this was the first true vampire story, unlike the folk tales or myths that had gone before.

THE CIVILIZED VAMPIRE

The Vampyre was the first story to introduce the idea of the vampire as being a civilized creature, perfectly capable of cunning and devious planning. Lord Ruthven was not, however, overly attractive; his skin had "a deadly hue" and his eyes were "dead grey."

His appeal seems to be more for his peculiarities than any physical attraction, and this less-than-healthy appearance was a feature of the vampires of the time, even to some extent the Master Vampire Dracula when we first meet him. The appeal of the vampire as a figure of mystery and intrigue really took off in the Victorian era, when tuberculosis was making real-life poets, such as Keats, look deathly pale and die young.

Victorian customs

This was partly because of the customs and rules of the time. Victorian women were expected to be demure, fragile, dependent on men, and most of all, not in the least interested in anything to do with physical love—and they certainly couldn't express it either. Their thoughts instead turned inward to fantasy, and the dark, brooding vampire easily became the focus of many women's dreams. As vampires weren't human, there was no need for the woman to feel she was betraying her husband. It's true that giving ourselves up for someone stronger than ourselves can be a powerful urge, and the vampire allows us to indulge our fantasies, but safely.

THE FEAST OF BLOOD →

An illustration from the penny-dreadful romance *Varney the Vampire*, 1847. Gaunt and pallid appearance notwithstanding, Varney uses his vampiric abilities to inveigle his way into the Bannerworth family and abuse their hospitality.

Aubrey and Ianthe

In the fashionable drawing rooms of London of the time there appears a man, Lord Ruthven, for whom beauty seems to have no effect. At this time Aubrey, an orphan with a decidedly romantic streak, also arrives in London. He makes Lord Ruthven's acquaintance, eventually arranging to travel with him on the Grand Tour of Europe.

As they travel, Aubrey gradually finds that, despite his apparent virtuous behavior in London, Lord Ruthven is given to vice and gambling. Being urged by his guardian, Aubrey travels to Greece, where he falls in love with Ianthe. One day, being warned that the wood is visited by vampires he plans to return from his excursion before sunset, but loses track of time and is caught in a storm. Hearing a woman's shrieks, he hurries to the hut from which the sounds come, but is himself attacked.

Interrupted by a search party with torches, his attacker flees, but Aubrey is distraught to find that the woman in distress is his beloved Ianthe, drained to death by a vampire.

Aubrey, sick at heart, returns home. To his horror he finds that his much-loved sister is due to be married to Earl Marsden, who is revealed to be the vampire Lord Ruthven!

Overcome by woe and disaster, Aubrey states what he knows. He dies straight afterward and messengers are sent to his sister. But they arrive too late.

"Lord Ruthven had disappeared, and Aubrey's sister has slaked the thirst of a VAMPYRE!"

FORBIDDEN PASSION

The vampire was portrayed as temptation in times when lust was a sin. The sophisticated, handsome vampire really came into his own in Victorian times, as a figure that repressed women could safely fantasize about.

Dracula Incarnations

THE ORIGINAL DRACULA

The story of Dracula was based on the historical character Vlad Drăculea (1431–1476), Prince and ruler of Romania during the 15th century. *Drăculea* meant "son of the dragon."

His father Vlad II had been a member of the Order of the Dragon, which required all those invested with the title to fight the enemies of Christianity and promote the Christian faith. Vlad Drăculea did, in fact, fight against the incursion of the Turkish empire into Romania, and was a hero, of sorts, to his people.

Organized chaos

When Vlad first came to power the country was in chaos and he set about ruthlessly organizing it from within in order to protect it from all its external enemies. He was successful, although his methods were often brutal. However in his defence this was a particularly brutal and violent period of history.

Ruthless cruelty

However, Vlad is perhaps best known for his extraordinary cruelty toward his enemies. He ordered that they were burnt, tortured, drowned, flayed alive, roasted, and boiled in huge vats. Some had their limbs hacked off, others were forced to eat parts of their own relatives or friends—and he spared no-one, regardless of age, sex, religion, or class.

Favorite method

His favorite method of execution, and the one for which he is best known, was impalement; a particularly slow and excruciatingly painful way to end one's days. He once, famously, ate his dinner in front of the battlefield scene of all his impaled enemies.

STOKER'S FAMOUS VERSION

Dracula by Bram Stoker, probably the most famous vampire story of all time, was first published in 1897. Although not the first vampire story ever written, *Dracula* is the book that truly sparked off the interest in vampires in the general public and formed the basis for the first well-known vampire films. It also threaded together the various traditions to create one "ultimate" vampire. The book is mainly composed of letters, newspaper clippings, new-fangled telegrams, journal entries, and anecdotes. This style keeps the reader personally involved all the way through.

CASTLE BRAN

Built in 1377, Castle Bran stands on the border of Transylvania and Wallachia. It's been said to have been Vlad Tepes's castle and also the inspiration for Castle Dracula in Stoker's book: unfortunately neither is true. However, it remains an iconic image, forever associated with the Dracula legend.

Harker's quest

The story is well-known: Jonathan Harker, a newly qualified solicitor, travels to Transylvania to assist Count Dracula in purchasing properties in England. On the way he is warned by the superstitious native peasants not to go to the castle, as it is an evil place owned by an evil man. Harker, keen to make his mark on his profession and prove himself a success on his first commission, ignores them. He does, however, accept a crucifix that someone gives him to keep him safe.

Although at first impressed with the Count's courteous manner, Harker soon realizes that he's way out of his depth: letters dictated by the Count to his superior and his fiancée, Mina Murray, make him fear for his life, a fear made worse when he is attacked by Dracula's three vampire brides. He does eventually escape the castle, but ends up very ill and weak at a monastery.

Dracula in England

Meanwhile Dracula has traveled to England on the ship *Demeter*, which arrives at the town of Whitby with its crew dead and the captain lashed to the wheel. As the ship hits the rocks off the coast, a great wolf leaps to the shore.

Wasting away

Not long afterward Dracula begins menacing Mina and her aristocratic friend Lucy Westenra. Lucy begins to waste away for no reason anyone can discover and Dr. Seward, the owner and manager of the nearby lunatic asylum, calls on his revered friend and tutor Professor Abraham Van Helsing, who is skilled in the study and treatment of exotic diseases. He recognizes it as the work of a vampire, being also versed in esoteric lore, but is reluctant to say anything because he thinks no one will believe him.

However, blood transfusions are clearly not helping. He has to return to Amsterdam briefly, and on that night Lucy is, apparently, killed. She is buried in "a lordly death-house in a lonely churchyard," but soon after reports of a "lady" stalking children causes Van Helsing to realize that his private diagnosis of vampirism was correct. He, Seward, and Lucy's two other suitors visit her grave, stake and behead her, and fill her mouth with garlic.

THE NEXT VICTIM

In the meantime, Mina has traveled to Budapest to be reunited with her fiancé. She and Harker are now married. They return to England, where Dracula, in revenge for Lucy's destruction, targets Mina as his next victim. He forces her to drink his blood, creating a mental and physical bond between them, and ensuring she will become a vampire after her death.

Dracula's demise

The only way to stop Mina's death is to kill Dracula. Under Van Helsing's hypnosis, Mina is able to tell her protectors that Dracula is fleeing to Transylvania: they follow and are able to catch him just before he reaches the safety of the castle. He is beheaded and stabbed through the heart. With his death, Mina is released and becomes fully human again.

Native American Vampire Legend

There was once a powerful Medicine Man who ruled wisely and kindly, and he loved the maiden Laughing Sky. They were wed and lived in peace and happiness save for one thing—Laughing Sky was barren; they had no son.

The Medicine Man prayed to the Great Spirit, but his prayers went unheard, and in time Laughing Sky was reaching the end of her child-bearing years. In desperation he declared that unless the Great Spirit granted him a son, he would no longer obey and serve, but still there was no answer.

The Medicine Man turned to darker and more forbidden arts, and opened a portal to usher in a powerful spirit from the realm of spirit shadows, Jumlin, who promised him many fine sons and daughters. But Jumlin lied and took over the heart and mind of the Medicine Man instead.

Jumlin was a strong and cruel spirit, who fed on the blood of living things. First he took the young braves to feed his appetites, then the women, then even the children. He sired many children, who were all born strong and healthy. His tribe, who had once loved the Medicine Man, grew to fear and hate him. They sent hunters to another tribe to learn how Jumlin could be destroyed, as the Medicine Man was no longer human and couldn't be killed by any normal means.

When they returned they found Laughing Sky very ill and close to giving birth. After Laughing Bear was born, Jumlin drained her blood, then escaped with his newborn son and several women of the tribe across the plain.

Laughing Bear grew as strong and cruel as his father, but one day the hunters caught them up. The Medicine Man and the demon within him were destroyed, but Laughing Bear escaped, and with his brothers and sisters he walks the Earth today, the first vampires, the cruel and vicious drinkers of blood.

Victorian appeal

Stoker spent years researching European folklore and legends of vampires before writing the book. Though not an immediate best-seller, the book was well received and went on to become an extremely successful play in Stoker's lifetime. On the face of it, it's a rollicking horror-adventure story in the Gothic style, but its real power lies in the then-shocking imagery of biting, blood, and the vampire's hypnotic power over women.

Vlad the Impaler

 The character of Dracula was modeled on a real person, Vlad Drăculea (see also page 84), who was born into a cruel, violent world colored by near-constant war and political intrigue. His country of birth, Transylvania, was the gateway between the Muslim Ottoman Empire and Christian Europe, and was a very dangerous place. Incursions by the Turks frequently led to widespread death and destruction—not just through war, but through the diseases they brought. They responded with the superstitious belief that demons were responsible.

At the age of five Vlad was initiated into the Order of the Dragon. Later, eligible for his apprenticeship into knighthood, he was taught archery, swordsmanship, court etiquette, and horsemanship. The politics of the time would have been Machiavellian, dictating that it was better for a ruler to be feared than loved, a notion that Vlad carried into his adult life.

Around 1437, threatened with invasion by the Turkish Empire, his father pledged to become a vassal of the Sultan and gave up Vlad and his younger brother, Radu, as hostages to his bond. As soon as he was old enough, Vlad served as an officer in the Turkish army, but ever after he nurtured a deep dislike and mistrust of his father and brother. After his father's murder in 1447, the Sultan installed Vlad on the throne as a puppet ruler, but in the same year John Hunyadi, regent of Hungary, invaded and deposed him. Vlad fled to Moldavia, to his uncle's court, then to Hungary, where he so impressed Hunyadi with his abilities that he was later proposed as a candidate for the throne of Wallachia. In 1456, after driving the Turks out of Wallachia, he finally took the throne of his own country.

It's not surprising that Vlad became the model for Bram Stoker's master vampire Dracula. His utter ruthlessness, his association with blood and cruelty, and his absolute control over those in his power makes the correlation a strong one.

Dracul originally meant "dragon." These days it has come to have the meaning "Devil" in Romania. How much of this is due to Vlad III's influence is open to debate!

THE IMPALER DINES OUT

This German woodcut, made in 1499, shows Vlad Drăculea, known as Voivode of Walachia, the Impaler, having a relaxing meal in the midst of the evidence of his renowned cruelty.

NOSFERATU

The first movie version of the Dracula book was *Nosferatu*, released 1921, directed by F.W. Murnau and starring Max Schreck as Graf Orlok.

The classic horror movie

Murnau had aimed to make a movie based on Bram Stoker's *Dracula*, however, after copyright issues with Stoker's widow, he renamed it *Nosferatu*, changed Dracula to Orlok and modified other details; this film is the result. It's silent and shot in black and white, of course, but it remains one of the classic horror films of all time. Max Schreck makes a truly eerie vampire; grotesque and malevolent. This is a far more chilling portrayal of the mythical bloodsucker than any other, before or since.

BELA LUGOSI

After Max Shreck's portrayal of the Dracula figure in *Nosferatu*, the next noteworthy depiction of the Master Vampire Dracula was Bela Lugosi in 1931. Now looking somewhat dated (sound was quite new), with clumsy, hammed-up acting, this version is nevertheless important for presenting

the Count as a suave, exotic nobleman rather than a physically ugly monster. There are no fangs displayed in the film, and the camera cuts away before any biting takes place, making it a lower-key version than most that came after it. This isn't too surprising given the times in which it was made; graphic details were considered far too shocking to be shown to the public. However, it is highly effective, adding an eerie atmosphere—the things we can't see can be more frightening than those we can. This is also the first film in which Dracula is shown sweeping his cloak up and out to hide his feeding, something that became fairly standard in subsequent films, especially the Hammer Horror series (see page 181).

Perfect for the role

Lugosi was Hungarian-born, and had the perfect accent for the part of Dracula. Tall, urbane, and handsome on screen, Lugosi's portrayal essentially set the standard for the cinematic portrayal of Dracula for the next few decades.

CHRISTOPHER LEE

Dracula (aka *Horror of Dracula*) was released in 1958. This was Christopher Lee's first appearance as Dracula and he went on to play the Count in another six films. Lee's height and regal good looks gave him great screen presence.

His Dracula was cool, commanding, and aristocratic: not a vampire one would dare to disobey, especially when he could turn extremely nasty when crossed. His vampire was as physical as any human, unable to shape-shift, but he was supernaturally strong, lacked a reflection, and

---

NOSFERATU, A SYMPHONY OF HORROR

A still from the 1921 movie *Nosferatu*, directed by Friedrich Wilhelm Murnau, showing Max Schreck in the starring role. A silent film, the actor is shown in full vampire regalia: whitened face, extended fingernails, and a long, black coat.

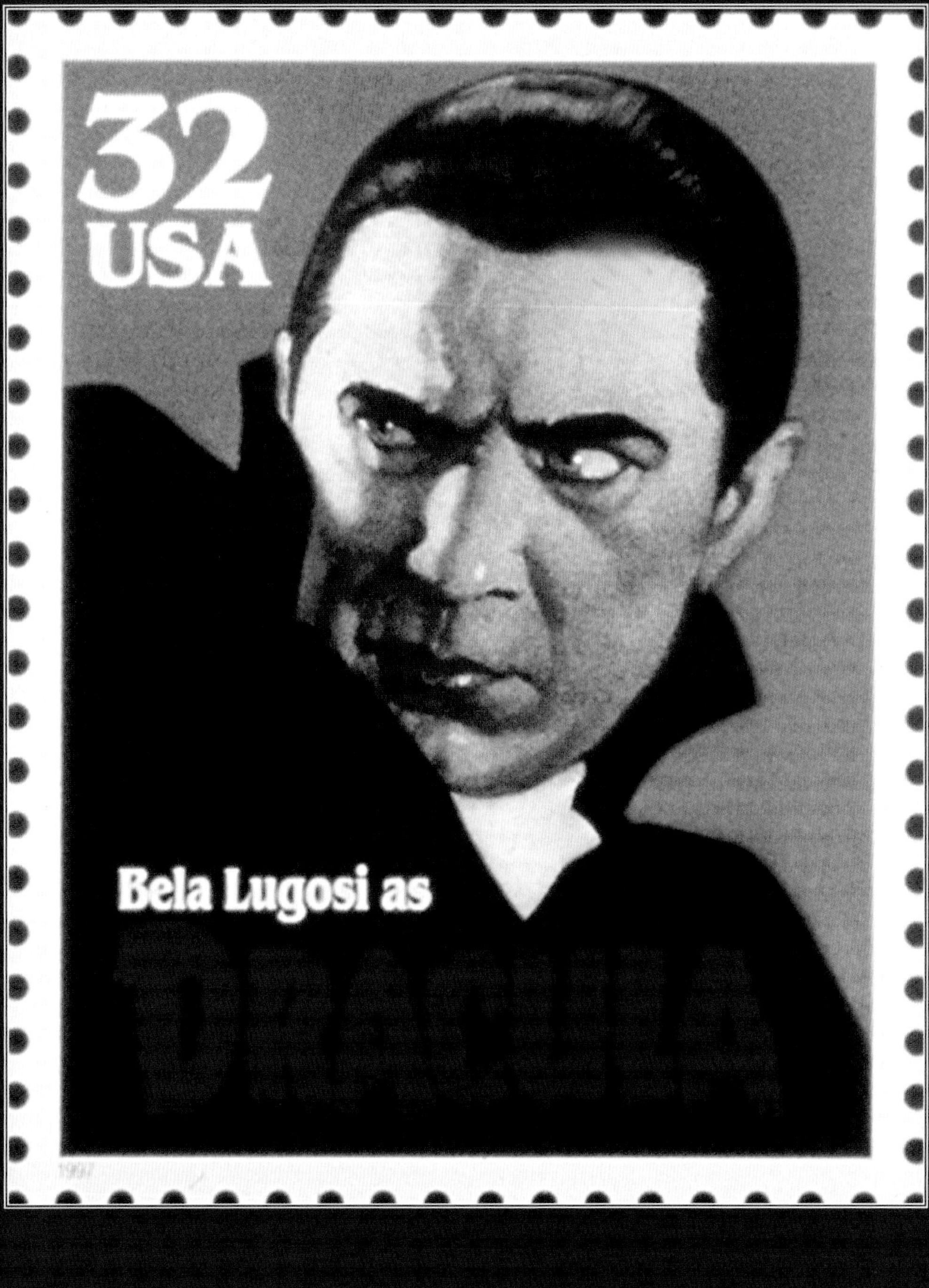
32
USA
Bela Lugosi as
DRACULA
1997

DRACULA STAMPED OUT

This US postal service stamp shows Dracula played by Bela Lugosi in the 1931 movie version. The Postal Service unveiled five movie monster stamps in that year in a ceremony at Universal Studios, California. The other stamps depicted Frankenstein, the Mummy, Wolfman, and the Phantom of the Opera.

FIRE AND PASSION

Frank Langella in the 1979 version of *Dracula*. Handsome, lithe, and cultured, this vampire's smoldering passion proved irresistible to women. He pursued his prey with an understated but powerfully flattering ruthlessness.

was unable to endure sunlight. The Count is portrayed as charming to begin with, but is quickly revealed to be a thoroughly evil creature. There is nothing we can find to sympathize with here: Dracula is simply a monster; first to be feared and then eventually destroyed.

FRANK LANGELLA

The 1979 Dracula, with Frank Langella as the Count, was a turning point in the evolution of the vampire from being portrayed as pure monster to being a seductive anti-hero: he was the first actor to give Dracula sex-appeal.

Smoldering

Langella was hypnotically charming as the Count: where Lugosi was sophisticated and Lee imposing, Langella smoldered. Being particularly good-looking helped, of course, to pave the way for later irresistible vampire characters.

Ruthless

However, charm didn't stop the Count from being ruthlessly evil, and he is still a predatory creature at heart, but we can empathize with his search for a woman strong enough to share the centuries with him. Both concepts—the vampire as a desirable creature and his wish for a permanent mate—became standard features in subsequent stories; in movies, books, and TV shows.

GARY OLDMAN

Oldman played Dracula in the 1992 film *Bram Stoker's Dracula*. Dracula here is shown to be Vlad III, the Impaler. Oldman's Count was an angry, troubled soul who had decisively turned his back on his savior when his wife, believing the Count killed in battle, committed suicide rather than live without him.

The very act of denying Christ caused the cross on the altar of the castle chapel to bleed while drinking the blood turned him into a vampire. This is an interesting inversion of the usual "eternal life" gained through symbolically drinking Christ's blood.

Complex creature

This vampire was able to walk in daylight, although it was less amenable to him than the darkness, was a shape-shifter, and as in Stoker's book, could move like a lizard or spider, able to creep head-first down a wall. He was a complex creature, capable of both extreme savagery and a tender, yearning love, both more terrifying and at the same time more sympathetic than any other Draculas that went before. He marked a turning point in our thinking about the modern vampire.

Of course, while Dracula will always be the Master Vampire, the character that inspired the vampires phenomenon of the 20th and 21st centuries, he wasn't the only one, nor, it can be argued, the best. As TV ownership became more widespread and TV programing more complex, the nature of the vampire changed and developed with the times.

DARK SHADOWS

Jonathan Frid played the tormented vampire, Barnabas Collins, in the ground-breaking, long-running serial *Dark Shadows*. The series chronicles the story of the Collins family of the fictional town of Collinsport, Maine.

The series played from 1966 to 1971, clocking up a mammoth 1,225 episodes. Originally it had no supernatural elements: ghosts were introduced six months into the series, bumping up the ratings, then six months after that, Barnabas Collins, the family vampire, made his appearance and the show's popularity soared.

Daring storylines

The storylines were melodramatic and daring for the time. With atmospheric setting, shifting timelines, and even time-travel plots, the

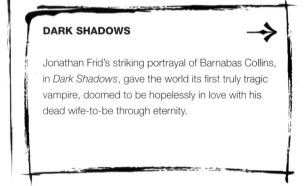

DARK SHADOWS

Jonathan Frid's striking portrayal of Barnabas Collins, in *Dark Shadows*, gave the world its first truly tragic vampire, doomed to be hopelessly in love with his dead wife-to-be through eternity.

characters were memorable and attractive, and the series became a cult classic.

Feeling sympathy

For the first time the viewing public was presented with a vampire for whom they could feel some sympathy. Barnabas had been made a vampire as an act of revenge by a slighted lover, rather than choosing his own fate, and was presented as a tragic figure. After his love and intended bride killed herself, he asked to be killed, but his father, unable to bear the thought of killing his son, instead had him sealed into a coffin and buried. There he remained for 175 years until accidentally

THE LOST BOYS

"Sleep all day. Party all night. Never grow old. Never die. It's fun to be a vampire." This was the first film to appeal truly to the younger generation. The Lost Boys lived and hunted together, their sex appeal balanced by the sheer ferocity of their feeding habits.

released by a treasure hunter. Trapped in a coffin for 175 year—death might have been kinder.

Star of the show

But instead of reacting violently, Barnabas remained his cultured, dignified, elegant self, forcing the viewer to respect and admire him, as well as finding him intensely compelling. He was only supposed to be in the series for 13 episodes, but the character proved to be so popular with audiences that he remained as a star of the show.

TEENAGE VAMPIRES

The Lost Boys, the 1987 vampire film starring Kiefer Sutherland and Jason Patric, was the first mainstream vampire film to make the undead deliberately appealing to younger cinema-goers. The vampires here are beautiful teenage leather-clad troublemakers, dark and dangerous, with an unpredictable edge, who ride powerful motorbikes. What's not to like?

Traditional but different

These vampires are cast in the traditional mold and sleep through the day, although their habit of hanging upside down from the roof, their elongated toes wrapped around the supports to hold them in place, is a fresh approach in vampire movies. Holy water will kill them if they are immersed in it for long enough. Their faces change when they hunt, becoming bestial and ugly: possibly the first time the effect was used in a vampire film; certainly the first time in a mainstream film. This allows them to pass in society when necessary and to look evil and monstrous when the occasion requires.

Two stages

In this film, becoming a vampire is a two-stage process. First the intended victim must drink from a bottle of aged vampire blood, at which point they become a half-vampire, with increased sensitivity to sunlight and an almost irresistible urge to sleep during the day. They do not, however, become a full vampire until they have made their first kill. They are also under the control of a Master Vampire, whose death will cause them to revert to human (or possibly die, if they are old). They are young, both in appearance and in attitude, rebellious, and immensely attractive to young humans (and a few older ones).

FOREVER KNIGHT

Nick Knight is the reluctant vampire and policeman in *Forever Knight*. Along with working for the police, he was trying to become human again, enlisting the help of the police coroner Dr. Brittington, who knew about his condition and did what he could to help, which included encouraging Nick to try eating food (which only made him sick), stop drinking blood (which he couldn't do since he couldn't survive without it, although he did take it from bottles rather than the neck), and use a tanning salon to try to combat his pallor (the sunbeds gave him claustrophobia and did nothing for his tan).

A sympathetic vampire

Among his vampiric talents, Nick was able to fly. He was one of the more sympathetic vampires, and while viewers might not have agreed with his wishes, they couldn't help admiring him for his principles. It was the first movie to place the vampire firmly on the side of good, showing that the creatures did not necessarily need to be evil, nor give in to their dark side. Nick gave a glimpse of what it means to be human from an outsider's point of view.

FROM THE VAMPIRE'S VIEWPOINT

Anne Rice's vampires made their debut in *Interview with the Vampire* (published in 1976, followed by the movie in 1994). Their story is told wholly from the vampire point of view.

Rice's vampires are traditional: they are made by drinking the blood of another vampire, are destroyed by sunlight, tend to kill their victims, and sleep in coffins, since this is the most effective way to exclude daylight. The books introduce the notion that once turned, a vampire cannot change at all, not even to cut off its hair: it simply grows back while they sleep. They are, as Josie says in *Being Human*, "Frozen. Like a photograph."

INTERVIEW WITH THE VAMPIRE →

Tom Cruise as Lestat de Lioncourt in Neil Jordan's *Interview With the Vampire* from 1994, based on the first book from Anne Rice's best-selling *Vampire Chronicles*, in which a vampire tells his life story. Lestat was the ultimate predator, a ruthless hunter who played with his prey like a cat with a mouse.

Boring undeath

Unlike some of their more recent brethren, however, these vampires often find undeath boring, and their immortality is spent constantly searching for something to fill up the loneliness.

Powerful, seductive, and hypnotic, Rice's vampires are especially dangerous. At least, some are. Lestat, in particular, is completely amoral, absolutely uncaring of almost anyone—but particularly of humans, who are nothing more than cattle to be fed upon—living entirely according to his own rules and literally doing anything he wants, with no moral sense to hold him back.

Child vampire

Lestat even commits what is almost the ultimate vampiric sacrilege and makes a vampire of a child, depriving Claudia of the chance to grow to womanhood and to experience all the normal joys of a human life.

Her mind and emotions develop so that they are a sort of warped version of adulthood, but her body remains that of a very young girl, and even the pleasure she obtains from the hunt isn't enough to sustain her. The sheer frustration of being trapped in a child's body only adds to her cruelty.

Lestat kills when he feeds, although it's clear that this is a matter of choice on his part: it's perfectly possible for vampires to limit their drinking to simply weaken the victim rather than drain them to death.

BUFFY

In the 1999–2004 spin-off of *Buffy the Vampire Slayer* we meet Angel, once the most vicious of vampires until a tribe of Kalderash Gypsies curses him by returning his human soul, thus giving him back his conscience and forcing him to confront all the evil he has done in his 145 years as a vampire. The guilt is overwhelming.

Fighting evil

Leading a troubled existence, trying to atone for his misdeeds, but usually failing, he is finally recruited to help Buffy fight evil. At several points he loses his soul and reverts to his previous evil self, but a little later regains his soul, thanks to the services of friends, and eventually creates Angel Investigations, dedicating himself to doing good and fighting demons.

The vampire with a soul

The notion of a vampire with a soul had never been addressed so overtly, and left the way open for considerations of what having a soul meant and how significant it might be in the greater scheme of things—to both humans and vampires.

THE VAMPIRE WITH A SOUL

Angel is Buffy's love interest throughout the first three seasons of *Buffy the Vampire Slayer* (see page 138). David Boreanaz plays the tortured vampire-with-a-soul Angel in the spin-off series in which he uses his powers to atone for evil done in his earlier life.

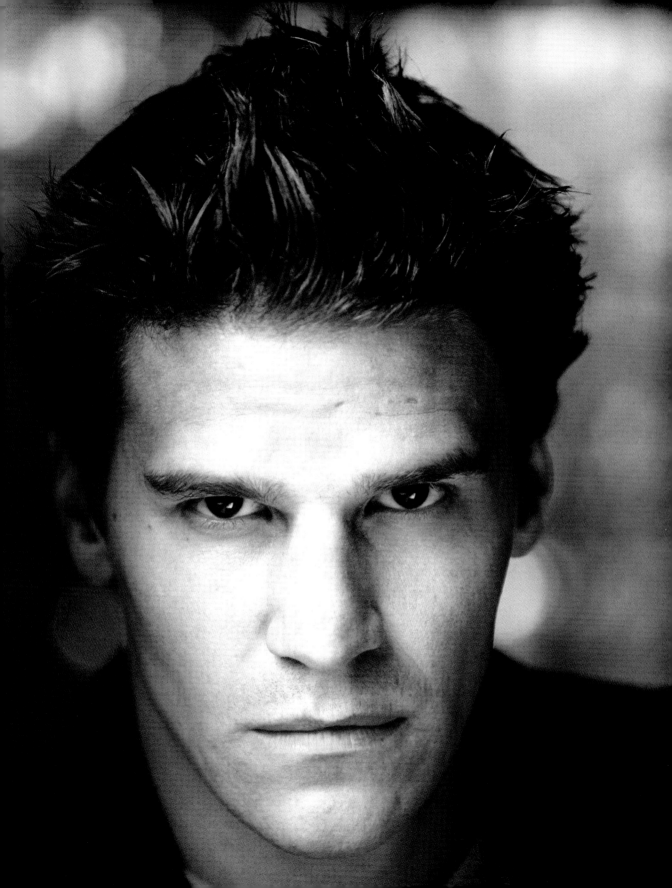

Angel is a relatively complex character, and appealingly human on occasion, his battles with his condition adding a poignancy to his actions.

THE MANSBRIDGE EXPERIMENT

Set in a world where vampires exist side-by-side with humans, although most humans don't know it, *Vampire High* deals with the Mansbridge Experiment.

Mansbridge Manor is an academy for students who've been expelled from every other college for rebellious and disturbed behavior. It's run by Dr. Murdoch, who treats his students firmly but fairly, encouraging them, generally successfully, to take responsibility for themselves and their actions. What the day students don't know is that he also runs the night school, which consists of a group of five very disparate "young" vampires who are being taught, reluctantly and against their natural inclinations, to live with, not on, the humans with whom they share the world.

The night school

The night students live in the cellar under the house and feed on medical blood supplies. Their lessons follow much the same course as those of the day school, but these students are much less easily controlled than the humans and the mortals are problematic enough! But they all persevere, knowing that the alternative could well be death for the vampires: the human world has its own vampire slayers.

The Mansbridge vampires remain wonderfully accessible once-humans, with their own

problems and desires that really aren't that different from their human counterparts. It is very easy to empathize with them and their struggle.

BLOOD TIES

In 2007 Kyle Schmid starred as the delectable Henry Fitzroy in the TV series *Blood Ties* (based on Tanya Huff's *Blood Books* series).

Henry Fitzroy is the illegitimate son of Henry VIII and currently a graphic novelist, who's been living quietly in Toronto for the past few years. Born in 1519 and now over 450 years old, Henry gives up his inheritance and his duty to his family in order to live forever with the woman he loves, the vampire Christina. But circumstances have parted them, and he has been forced to live without her, traveling the world as fate dictated.

The honorable vampire

Henry Fitzroy is what could best be called an honorable vampire. He admits that he has killed in the past and will kill in the future; it's part of what he is. But he controls the dark side of his nature, both to protect his existence and because it's far more pleasant taking what's offered than taking by force. He's intelligent and compassionate, and beautiful in a deliciously masculine way: combined with the manners and skills he's learned over nearly half a millennium; it makes him irresistible.

BEING HUMAN

Perhaps the most tragic and appealing vampire to date is Mitchell, one of the stars of the 2009 UK TV series *Being Human*. The series concerns the

The Vampire Cat of Japan

The Prince of Hizen has a favourite consort, O Toyo. After spending an evening in pleasant dalliance with her master, O Toyo retires for the night, not noticing that a cat has followed her. During the night the cat grows to a gigantic size and strangles her, afterward dragging the body off into the countryside, where it buries her, then takes her place as the Prince's consort.

The Prince falls ill, and grows weak and pale. It is suspected that he is suffering from some sort of demonic attack, so advisors and doctors are assigned to watch over him while he sleeps. However, they always fall asleep and so miss seeing the assault.

Eventually the Prince's loyal subject, the Buddhist Ito Soda, volunteers to guard him. Staying awake where the others had fallen asleep, Ito Soda sees O Toyo enter the Prince's bedchamber in the dark hours of the night. Seeing the Buddhist watching, however, she simply smiles and leaves the room again.

This happens over several nights, until O Toyo appears to lose interest in the Prince, ignoring him even during the day, and he begins to recover. Ito Soda approached O Toyo in her rooms, to accuse her of being the cause of the Prince's condition, whereupon she attacked him with a halberd. He managed to fight her off, and she escaped through the window.

A happy escape for the Prince, but then the cat began to attack the people of the surrounding mountains, and he was forced to raise a hunt for the creature. Finally it was caught and killed, and peace restored to the land.

lives of three housemates; a ghost, a werewolf, and a vampire, and deals with the problems and trials they face in their daily lives.

Happy flatmates

Mitchell, the Irish vampire, works as an orderly at Bristol General Hospital with George, the sweet but socially inept Jewish werewolf. They live in a rented house in Bristol, England, with the confused and unhappy ghost Annie. Mitchell doesn't burn in sunlight, but he is happier at night and prefers dark or cloudy days. He does, however, cast no reflection in anything silver-backed, such as a mirror or film.

He is able to eat normal food and drink, but needs blood to remain strong, and although he has sworn off feeding from humans, sometimes the compulsion becomes too powerful, taking him over.

Trying to be human

Allowing himself to be turned back in World War II in order to save his men, Mitchell has refused to join the main mass of vampires, preferring to be "clean" (not drink human blood) and trying desperately to exist as a human. The stories of all three of the friends are heartbreaking, but Mitchell's is more so than the others as he's faced every day with temptation, fighting his natural urges, struggling with the physical weakness that resisting drinking blood brings with it, and trying so hard to be accepted. As is not uncommon with modern vampires, he tries to make amends for previous mistakes.

Inner demons

We all have our demons to fight: Mitchell's just happen to be bigger and stronger than most of them. We can't help but feel deeply for him. And with that, the vampire becomes the boy next door, still dangerous if you catch him at the wrong time, but now approachable, sympathetic, and infinitely lovable.

TWILIGHT

The vampires in the *Twilight* series are so far removed from the traditional perception of the undead as to be a different species altogether. They exist solely on blood and have the speed and strength of the traditional vampire, only more so, but that's where the similarity ends.

Impossible beauty

These vampires are impossibly beautiful, with eyes that change color, depending on how recently they've fed, and skin that sparkles in the Sun. This is the only reason why they stay in the shade and live in places where they can be sure of a constant cloudy, overcast atmosphere.

They move with unbelievable speed and are immensely strong. Their flesh is cold and as hard as marble, making them distinctly uncomfortable to touch or hold; and their senses are extra-ordinarily enhanced. They never sleep. These vampires are loosely bound by rules dictated by the Volturi, the very ancient Italian vampires, who have made it their business to keep the existence of their kind secret from the human world.

Obsession

Edward Cullen, the vampire that the human female protagonist Bella is obsessed with, is alternately similarly obsessed with her or trying to stay away from her, as he's afraid his bloodlust will hurt her. He is extremely protective of her, which is probably just as well, since she has a talent for getting herself into trouble, and while she wants to become a vampire, he is very reluctant and worried about her losing her soul. Edward is concerned about the state of his own soul, too, unsure as to whether vampires possess them or not. Eventually he is forced to turn her, to save her life.

A STILL FROM TWILIGHT →

A girl risks everything when she falls in love with a vampire. A modern Romeo and Juliet story of the ultimate forbidden love affair between vampire and mortal. In this scene Isabella, awed by her feelings for Edward and his for her, tries to convince him to turn her so that they may spend eternity together.

Vampire Summary

VAMPIRE TYPES

It is useful to distinguish between the several different sorts of vampire. There may, of course, be overlaps in types. For example, a noble vampire may also be an elder as well, while a feral can also be a lonely type.

Traditional vampire

The traditional vampire burns in the Sun, drinks blood frequently and in considerable quantity, and often has no reflection in mirrors. He is very strong and fast, and may be averse to religious icons, although this shouldn't be taken for granted. He may be able to shape-shift and become mist, however, this ability seems to be growing rarer as centuries pass. He invariably sleeps through the day, usually in a coffin and often on a bed of his native earth. He can be killed by staking, burning, or beheading, and he is usually but not always a loner, often ruthless in achieving his goals.

Daywalker vampire

The traditional daywalker vampire has the same limitations, but is able to walk in daylight, whether because sunlight does not harm him, or because, like Saint-Germain, he has learned to line his shoes with native earth, which protects him. Usually ancient, wise, and learned, he has a deep appreciation of life and rarely takes it unless in self-defence. He drinks only enough to sustain his life: it is often the trust and love of the giver that nourishes him far more than the actual blood. Religious icons usually have no power over such a being. This type of vampire is rare, but desirable. The modern daywalker has very few traditional limitations, is equally at ease in daylight or at night, and can almost pass for human while retaining vampiric strength and power. They can be the most dangerous of all.

Noble vampire

The noble vampire is often old and knowledgeable, usually only requiring a little blood to continue existence. He enjoys the finer things in life and is courteous toward humans, accepting blood only from those disposed to give it. Religious icons may be ineffectual.

Older vampire

The elder vampire holds power over his family, clan, or brood, and rules ruthlessly. He is often a businessman, ruling his organizations from a

DESTRUCTIVE SUNLIGHT

In the 1921 version of *Nosferatu*, Max Shreck, as Count Orlok, is destroyed by sunlight. This silent movie is haunting testament to the power of the vampire legend, and a striking example of limited resources resulting in a lasting work of art. The Count is truly one of the most memorable vampires ever.

distance—a shadowy but forceful executive figure who few ever see.

Feral vampire

The feral vampire is only interested in blood and violence. He may be relatively intellectual and disciplined, or he may simply be wild, but he is always extremely dangerous and completely amoral. He's also unpredictable: the usual limitations may have no effect whatsoever on him. This type of vampire usually lives in a pack.

Lonely vampire

The lonely vampire could be considered a special case. Many vampires enjoy their condition, or at least have become resigned to it. The lonely vampire, however, hates what he is and fights against it at all times, angry and bitter at the world—and particularly at the vampire who turned him—and refuses to accept that this is all there is. Such a vampire can, on occasion, commit suicide, usually by allowing himself to be caught during sunup.

UNDERWORLD →

Bill Nighy as the vampire Viktor the Elder in *Underworld: Evolution* (2006). We may not like him, nor the things he has done in the name of the vampire species, but we can't fault his loyalty or bravery. Always at the forefront of the battle, his savage dedication to his cause could be terrifying.

Here Come The Vamps!

Although the modern vampire tends to be male, the original vampiric creatures were mostly female. They were fiends who haunted the night, preying on pregnant women or small children, or luring travelers to their doom. Perhaps they were victims themselves; women who had died in childbirth or lost a newborn baby. Although they were horrific by nature, they were often portrayed as physically attractive.

Women and blood

In a way it's not surprising that the first vampires were female. Blood and women have always been intertwined, simply because of women having monthly periods. Perhaps women weren't to be trusted, purely because they could bleed for five days without dying.

To the primitive mind, this may have been a source of fear and awe, and would have made women seem both powerful and unearthly. This, in itself, may have been a reason why men felt the need to demean and control women, and brand them as monsters. It may also have been the reason why the original blood-suckers were seen as female: they needed to drink blood to replace what they'd lost.

An easy excuse

The belief that female vampires preyed on other women and children was a convenient excuse, easily supported: after all, women, especially pregnant women and malnourished children, are prone to fatigue, weakness, and anemia, and while we know the medical causes of such things these days, in ancient times it seemed only sensible to blame it on a demon of some sort.

As belief in vampires progressed, the few notable female vampires came to be seen as at least as powerful as their male counterparts; occasionally more so. The horrific tale of Countess Elizabeth Báthory's sadistic murders added to the image of the vampire as a noble, feudal monster living off the lifeblood of her subjects.

A REAL-LIFE VAMPIRE

Countess Elizabeth Báthory (1560–1614) was considered to be a real-life vampire. It was claimed she tortured and killed hundreds of young women and girls; as many as 600 according to one account. While this may be an exaggeration, she was certainly convicted on 80 counts, for which she was imprisoned in her castle, bricked up in her rooms until her death four years later.

Blood baths

The most famous legend surrounding Elizabeth's life is that she bathed in her victims' blood to maintain her youth and beauty, but this is more than likely a myth. It does seem, however, that as well as the sadistic thrill of the torture, she may have drunk her victims' blood.

Báthory Erzsébet 1570—1614

Čachtice. Sborenina

MINA: DRACULA'S VICTIM

In the tongue-in-cheek horror movie *The League of Extraordinary Gentlemen*, Mina, who was Dracula's victim in the original Bram Stoker book and subsequent films, was not cleansed of Dracula's blood when the Count was killed, but became what can only be a sort of dhampir. She does drink blood when it's called for, in self-defence for example, is very strong and fast, heals almost instantaneously and, delightfully, can change into a flock of bats, but she can walk in the sunshine and apparently doesn't need to drink blood regularly to stay alive. She is wonderfully aristocratic and aloof without being arrogant, and

ELIZABETH BÁTHORY

Popularly nicknamed the Blood Countess, Elizabeth was an intelligent and educated woman. In her younger days she was said to have helped several women less fortunate than herself. We can only speculate as to what happened to change her into the monster she later became.

Laura & Carmilla

Laura lives with her father, a retired and wealthy English widower, in a castle in a forest in Austria. Although happy, she is often lonely and wishes for someone to be her companion. At the age of six she dreams of a beautiful girl in her bedchamber, and 12 years later a carriage accident near the castle brings the same girl into Laura's life. Carmilla, as the girl is called, claims to have had the reverse dream, in which Laura appeared in her bedroom. Carmilla's mother has urgent business and asks Laura's father to care for Carmilla for the three months it will take her to manage matters, to which the father agrees.

Laura and Carmilla become firm friends, although there are a number of things that Laura finds increasingly disturbing. Carmilla has a tendency to make sexual advances toward her new friend, sleeps most of the day, won't reveal anything about her family or past, and appears to sleepwalk at night. Laura's alarm grows when a restored family heirloom painting of the Countess Mircalla Karnstein is returned to the castle and is the absolute image of Carmilla.

After a while Laura starts to have dreams about a cat-like creature entering her room at night and biting her breast. She begins to feel ill and starts to waste away.

The family enlists the help of Baron Vordenburg, the descendent of the man who originally cleared the area of vampires, and with his ancestor's notes he is able to find and destroy the ancient vampire countess.

Carmilla by Joseph Sheridan Le Fanu, first published 1872.

THE LEAGUE OF EXTRAORDINARY GENTLEMEN

In Stoker's book, Mina was "cured" of her approaching vampirism when Dracula was killed. In the 2003 film, Mina wasn't cured but became a dhampir, retaining much of her human nature, and proved to be a staunch and powerful ally.

fully capable of holding her own against all the testosterone-fueled males around her. She is the absolute antithesis of the fragile Victorian flower one might expect of the time.

SELENE

The Death Dealer vampire Selene in *Underworld* and *Underworld Evolution*, is centuries old, beautiful, cool and emotionless, and a ruthless killer. Typically for a vampire, her age has enhanced her strength and invulnerability, along with her healing powers. She becomes intrigued

The Right Stuff

 Blood is responsible for carrying oxygen and nutrients to every part of the body, and for carrying wastes away. Without it, and without enough of it, we simply couldn't exist. It is 90 percent plasma, which itself is 55 percent plain water. The other 45 percent consists of various hormones, proteins, glucose, amino acids, and those all-important antibodies that protect us from disease. The 10 percent of blood that isn't plasma consists of the red blood cells that transport oxygen and the white blood cells that are a vital part of our immune systems. There are also platelets that clot the blood after injury, thus stopping us bleeding to death from a simple cut.

Blood is created in our bone marrow, oxygenated by our lungs, and pumped around our bodies by our hearts. It keeps us at the right temperature, and it's essential for the brain to be constantly supplied with freshly oxygenated blood: it only takes about four minutes for irreversible damage to be done to the brain if the heart stops pumping blood. It even comes in flavors: positive and negative O, A, B, and AB!

Unfortunately, despite its wonderful efficiency at keeping us alive—or perhaps because of it—blood is also a very useful way for viruses or parasites to colonize our bodies, and for toxins to spread through them. And that's where the vampire comes in. By taking the blood of a human and replacing it with his own, he infects his prey, and, like a virus that multiplies at a furious rate to overwhelm healthy blood cells, his contagion takes hold, mutating the victim into a vampire herself.

by, then attracted to, and later falls in love with, human Michael Corvin. Unfortunately he is then bitten by a Lucian, the head werewolf, meaning he will also turn become one. But Selene hates werewolves and has devoted her life to killing them after they destroyed her family (or so she is told by Viktor, the vampire who turned her). How she deals with the emotional turmoil forms much of the story. Selene is a strong character, willing to disobey authority in order to be true to herself.

UNDERWORLD: EVOLUTION

Actress Kate Beckinsale stars as Selene in the Len Wiseman-directed horror thriller *Underworld: Evolution*, released in 2006. Beautiful, powerful Selene, vampire Death Dealer, her destiny is to become the savior of her people—though she has to go through hell to get there.

Femme Fatale — Human Vamp

 Ideals of female beauty have changed through the ages. In times when food was scarce or hard to come by, large, very well-padded women were considered beautiful: they were healthy and obviously wealthy enough, whether by themselves or through their family or spouse, to keep well fed. In more recent times, in the Western world, anorexically thin has been decreed by the fashion industry to be the ideal. Neither extreme is particularly healthy, of course, and it's a wise person who doesn't allow themselves to be swayed by the vagaries of what other people think they should be like.

There is one icon of female beauty, however, that transcends body shape or fashion, and that's the femme fatale—otherwise known as the "vamp." Vamp is a state of mind rather than a physical appearance. It's a deep belief in one's own attractiveness, a sublime self-confidence married to an acceptance of one's imperfections.

Morticia Addams isn't actually a vampire, although she dresses and seems like one. She is a long way from the blonde perkiness that is often called "beautiful" in Western culture, but her physical appearance is stunning, and she takes her allure for granted. She makes no apology for what she is, even when that seems odd or perverted. She has an extraordinary

grace, and others naturally seem to defer to her. She takes their worship for granted. Her perception of morality is often at odds with the moral guidelines of her culture.

There have been a number of famous vamps down the centuries—or perhaps that should be infamous, as the fatale part of femme fatale can be very accurate; the vamp often uses her seductive charms to manipulate men. The list of legendary vamps is very long, from Lilith and Salome of Biblical times, through Cleopatra and Morgan le Fay, to the vamps of silent films—actresses like Theda Bara and Pola Negri. The female characters of such films as *Fatal Attraction* and *Basic Instinct* are more recent vamps, as is Persephone in *The Matrix* and *Matrix Reloaded*. The most famous real-life vamp was Mata Hari, exotic dancer and courtesan, accused of being a double agent during World War II.

THE PERFECT MORTICIA

Anjelica Huston as Morticia Addams is the perfect image of the vamp, commanding extraordinary presence in this alluring role.

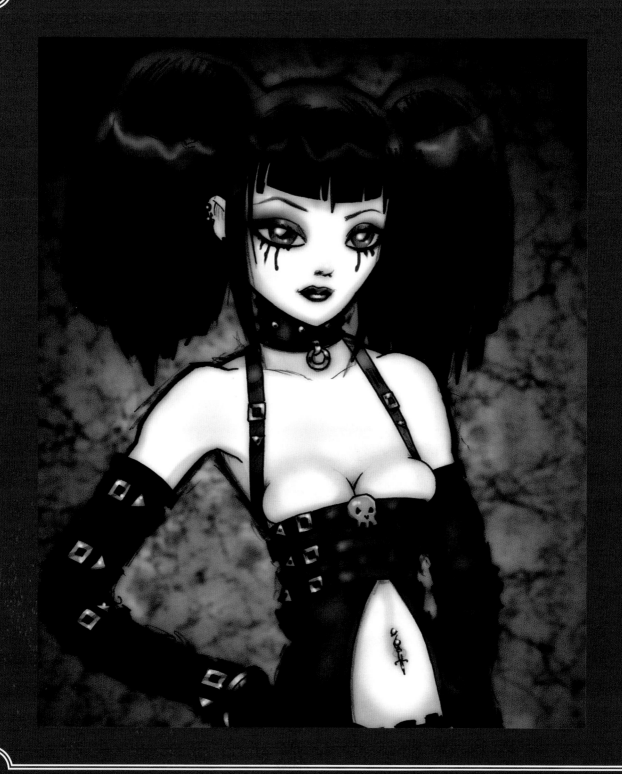

Chapter 4

Vampires &
Popular Culture

Vampire–Vampyre Style

ALTERNATIVE LIFESTYLES

There have been plenty of "alternative lifestyle" cultures in the past few decades; at least one or two main ones every ten years or so.

There were the mods and rockers of the late 1950s and early 60s, the hippies of the late 1960s, the punks of the late 1970s, the New Romantics of the early 1980s, while the 1990s saw an explosion of lifestyles as the World Wide Web made the fashions and music of the whole world available to everyone with an Internet connection. Of all the alternative lifestyles, the goth subculture has been very long-lived: it started in the early 1980s and is still going strong.

Longing to belong

At heart, anyone belonging to any such lifestyle does so for one, or more, of several different reasons. Firstly, they may have an emotional link to the underlying beliefs of the lifestyle: anti-war, pro-peace movement in the case of the hippy; rebellion and anarchy for punks; an interest in horror movies, gothic literature, and a gloomy esthetic in the case of the goth.

An individual may feel so strongly about their beliefs that they want to proclaim them through their dress and behavior. They may simply be rebelling against what they see as "authority," in which case their allegiance may switch over time. Or they may just like the look of the clothes,

> ### A GROUP OF GOTHS →
>
> A major characteristic of the goth and vampire culture is black clothes, occult jewelry, and pale makeup. The goth scene is largely centered around Germany these days, though it has enthusiastic followers worldwide.

jewelry, and other bits and pieces that go with the lifestyle. Of particular interest to the West was the influence of the Japanese Lolita subculture, with its emphasis on Victorian doll-like little girls.

VAMPIRES AND VAMPYRES

There is a distinction between "vampire" and "vampyre," and between the two lifestyles. "Vampyre" lifestyle is often seen as an overlap with the goth subculture, and the two have quite a lot in common.

Vampires

A vampire ("real" vampire) may be the person next door. They may dress the part, or they may prefer to remain anonymous, but they have a deep personal belief that they are really a vampire, a separate species from humanity. This is the Human Living Vampire discussed on pages 46–7.

Vampyres

Vampyre lifestylers, however, are all about living the vampire esthetic. Elegance, detachment, and often a certain studied look of boredom, are required personal traits. Vampyre lifestylers dress and act the part, and decorate their homes accordingly. There are some who go as far as to sleep in their own coffin, with the lid up, one hopes, unless there are airholes for easy breathing, although the cost is probably beyond most vampyres, and not really recommended for anyone with claustrophobia. Their homes are usually darkly elegant and baroque, frequently with Victorian or "Renaissance" decorations: black lace and candles are often a feature, and bats, fangs, and images of the moon may also be seen. A solemn, even gloomy, atmosphere is considered appropriate, and lighting is subtle and atmospheric with the addition of heavy drapes.

Look the part

Vampyre clothes are always dark in color, predominantly black, but often with red or rich purple accents. The style of clothes tends to be historical in style: loosely "Victorian," "Medieval," or "Renaissance," with long skirts,

Vampyre Threads

 To be a real goth or vampyre it's vital to look the part and this means wearing the right clothes and accessories.

There are a number of stores and outlets catering to goths in general, and vampires in particular, around the world. Here is a small selection:

Boutique de Vampyre in New Orleans, USA, is one of the most famous. Their online store is currently at www.feelthebite.com, but if things change in the digital age, a search engine enquiry should be able to find them fairly easily. The **Black Angel** is a truly international online store, catering for the global goth and vampyre. **Vampire UK** is an excellent resource for the UK vampire: find them at www.vampire.co.uk. London has the **Darkside** store in Camden, and St Nicholas' Market (established in the 1740s) in Bristol, home of *Being Human*, contains Twilight Fashions. Most large cities have at least one alternative lifestyle outlet, although you might have to dig a little to find it!

high-necked blouses, shawls, hats and veils, calf-length boots, and flowing dresses with lacy petticoats. Some vampyres wear close-fitting, revealing clothing such as corsets, long, tight skirts, and lace trimmings, epitomizing the popular image of the "vamp" or in imitation of legendary figures.

Vampyre adornment

Favorite goth and vampyre jewelry tends to be either large, chunky and macabre, or more refined and delicate, usually made from silver and black crystal, although blood-red or purple stones or crystals are also hot favorites. Crosses are a popular symbol, as is anything Victorian, and chokers add the right finishing touch to a slender throat. Some vampyres like blood jewelry; tiny "glass" vials, some fang-shaped, test-tubes or teardrops containing blood. The blood can be fake, or, for the true lifestyler, the vial can be filled with real blood—their own or that of a friend or lover.

Pale complexions

Makeup tends to pale the complexion with dark and dramatic eyes and black or blood-red lips. Nails are usually long and beautifully manicured, with black or red varnish. Vampyre-lifestyler hair is usually long, thick and dramatic, black or red, and often worn in a splendid cascade of curls. The overall look is one of elegance and drama. Tattooing and piercing can carry over from goth to vampyre, but may not be considered to be a part of the esthetic: too much piercing is anything but elegant and can spoil the overall grace and solemnity of the vampyre look. There are, however, some very attractive vampyre tattoos around, and a discreet design can be appealing, especially if it's applied to an area that's not constantly on show. However, since tattoos are there for ever, it may be more advisable to use the wide range of temporary versions available. Bear in mind that there are age limits for permanent tattooing and piercing.

Teeth and eyes

Some dedicated lifestylers go as far as to have their teeth capped to look like fangs: there are a number of advertized dental-work specialists prepared to do this, but it's wise to make sure the professional is properly qualified before making any such medical changes. Again, this is for adults only. Colored contact lenses are also favored. These come in an almost unlimited range of colors and patterns, but for the vampyre crimson, purple, or black are usually the best choices, although brilliant, emerald green or gold can look stunning with an elegant black outfit. It's always advisable to get an optician's advice first, in case of any medical problems.

Vampyre sounds

Music is a vital part of the goth scene, and is important to the vampyre lifestyle as well. While some vampyres enjoy traditional goth music: Gothic Rock, Dark Rock, and Industrial, for example, many prefer the possibly more melodic music of bands such as Inkubus Sukubus,

Nosferatu, and Blood Lust. For the more discriminating lifestyler, classical music is often the better choice, fitting in as it does with the vampire esthetic.

REAL OR FAKE?

Lifestylers are sometimes viewed by "real" vampires as fakes, only interested in the outward trappings of the vampire life. They pretend to be vampires, but have none of the spiritual, physical, or psychic experiences or abilities of the real thing. They may also be seen as attracting too much attention to the whole vampire lifestyle, making it more difficult for the "real" vampire to remain anonymous.

FINDING OUT MORE

Anyone interested in finding out more about the vampyre lifestyle should type "international vampire associations" into their search engine. There are a huge number of links to associations all over the world: finding one nearby should be quite straightforward. Alternatively, a lot of information can be found in vampire magazines.

A good magazine

There are quite a few of these online, but a very good paper version is *Bite Me: the Journal of the Vampire and Its Kin*. Started in 1999 in the UK, this glossy, information-packed magazine can be ordered online. As well as fashion, music, and film articles, it contains interviews, reviews, art and fiction, news of upcoming bands and films, and some very unusual and intriguing articles such as that on the horses that sweat blood in Issue Twenty.

Vampire: Playing Games

Vampyre lifestylers, in many cases, join the lifestyle through getting involved with role-playing games (RPG) such as *Vampire: the Masquerade/Requiem,* or from a deep wish to emulate the heroes of vampire literature, most often Anne Rice's characters.

However, it should be stressed that RPG players (or "gamers") are not necessarily vampyre lifestylers, and are far more into the RPG than in pretending to be vampires specifically. Many also enjoy playing mages, werewolves, elves, orcs, zombies, warriors, and many other fantasy characters and creatures.

ROLE-PLAYING

In 1991, *Vampire: the Masquerade,* the first *World of Darkness* role-playing game, made its appearance. Not unlike the first true RPG, *Dungeons and Dragons, Vampire: the*

Vampire Clans in Masquerade

The Masquerade provides the outward appearance of normality that allows the vampires to live and thrive in the human community. Each vampire belongs to a clan:

➤ *Brujah/Bruja The rebels; the anarchists. Independent, outspoken, passionate, and often violent or criminally minded. They consider change a good thing; essential to survival and evolution.*

➤ *Gangrel The loners; the survivors. They are self-reliant and individualistic warriors, often seen as uncivilized; they are shape-shifters.*

➤ *Malkavian The psychics, possessing strange and unpredictable powers. They are also technically insane.*

➤ *Nosferatu They are physically ugly, resembling the actor Max Schreck in the film Nosferatu. They are the essential spymasters and secret gatherers, selling vital information to the other clans.*

➤ *Toreador The aristocratic, glamorous, and beautiful artists and creators. More than any other clan they depend upon the "masquerade," grace, and civilized behavior, to maintain their relations with the human world. They are also very often shallow and selfish.*

➤ *Tremere Secretive and meticulously well-organized, they are the warlocks and magic-workers of the Camarilla.*

➤ *Ventrue The oldest, most venerable clan; the overlords and the leaders of the Kindred.*

Masquerade is a variety of storytelling. Indeed, the games master is called the Storyteller. More recently the Masquerade book and system has been replaced with *Vampire: the Requiem* (produced by the same company). Though some rules and clans have changed slightly, the two games are very similar and take place in much the same fantasy universe.

The role of RPGs

RPGs involve a gathering of like-minded people who assume the personalities of characters in the game to act out scenarios determined by the Storyteller. Unlike competitive board or card games, RPGs need the players' interaction and cooperation to be successful. In the game, the players take the characters of, naturally, vampires, who refer to themselves collectively as the "Kindred." The parent organization is called the Camarilla, and keeps the Masquerade going.

Torpor

In this section only sunlight or decapitation can kill a vampire, while a stake through the heart sends them into a torpor—sleep which can last for centuries. Other things that induce torpor are when a vampire becomes too old or insane to continue, or when they have been denied blood for a long time. Torpor is preferable to starvation—in which the vampire attacks the nearest food source, regardless of risk, though they may not have a choice.

Taking different forms

Some vampires in this game can take the form of animals, such as bats or wolves, or can turn into a pool of blood, while others can use magic, telepathy, mist, or make illusions.

The game is intensely political, revolving around the different characters' various allegiances to clans and philosophies. To date, the group RPG has spawned a video game, an online version in moderated chat forums, a computer game (*Vampire: the Masquerade—Bloodlines*), a series of graphic novels, and a 1996 TV series, *Kindred: the Embraced*.

Eating up your time

To find out more about the phenomenon, type "white-wolf.com" or "vampire: the masquerade" into your browser's search engine, but be warned; *Vampire: the Masquerade* and its follow up *Vampire: the Requiem* are massively intricate and complex games, and will eat up your time if you let them.

Similar games

There are other similar, overlapping games by the White Wolf games company, including *Werewolf: The Apocalypse*, and *Kindred of the East*, which is peopled with Asian vampires; quite different in form, history, and powers from their Western counterparts, but it's an interesting alternative for anyone wishing to try a different perspective.

Kindred: the Embraced

 The mid-90s TV series, *Kindred: the Embraced* gained enormous popularity. Several fascinating themes were explored and developed.

For many centuries the Kindred lived openly among humans, flaunting their powers and abilities, until the Inquisition, when the Church rounded up and burned all those they considered unholy: heretics, vampires, werewolves, witches, the accused, and recent converts, who were under a great deal of suspicion. They also captured anyone who posed a threat and were dangerous to the Church-established order.

Thereafter, the supernatural creatures of the world lived in hiding, the vampire clans coming together under the protection of the Camarilla.

The "masquerade" refers to the game the vampires have to play in order to appear human to the people with whom they share the world, while also remaining true to their own selves. As main character Julian Luna says in Episode Two, "We stay safe from humans by staying close to them. We keep our enemies closest."

The Kindred have several useful talents: they can endure sunlight if they've recently fed, shape-shift into wolves and birds of prey, principally owls, and they are psychometric, able to relive events from the past by holding something that someone else has touched.

The act of turning a human is called "embracing": the humans who are turned are called the Embraced. As with traditional vampires, embracing involves draining the human to the very point of death and then feeding them on vampire blood, so that they create a bond between Embraced and Sire. Embracing requires the permission of the Prince of the City, however, and the Prince is entitled to destroy both the Embraced and the blood drinker Sire if permission isn't sought.

The vampires in the series, as in the game, are ordered into a clearly defined hierarchy with fairly strict rules, and with constant tension as the different clans form temporary alliances and get involved in feuds.

They interact very much as human societies and cultures do, but in microcosm, allowing for a more intimate exploration of characters.

Vampires & Werewolves

EXAMPLES IN FICTION

Werewolves and vampires are popularly depicted as being mortal enemies, though there are a few exceptions. *Kitty and the Midnight Hour*, for example, is the first volume of the fascinating tale of Kitty Norville, the young radio station host and first-ever werewolf to go public, on air, no less.

Coexistence

Although the book is mainly concerned with werewolves and werewolf society, the local pack coexists with the local vampire pack. It's not a particularly friendly coexistence, and the two species fight if they trespass on each others' agreed territory. However things are relatively peaceful, and the two alpha males, Carl the werewolf and Arturo the vampire, meet to discuss mutual problems and agree protocols for dealing with each other.

The tension between the two is, no doubt, not helped by the fact that to the vampires, werewolf blood is a particularly delicious delicacy. Kitty describes it as tasting like thirty-year-old whiskey, or something equally aged and succulent— definitely a luxury that would be extremely tempting to a vampire.

Cute werewolves

In the second of Tanya Huff's *Blood Books, Blood Trail*, we meet the teenage twins Peter and Rose, or Storm and Cloud in their "fur-form," perhaps the cutest pair of werewolves in existence. They and their pack and vampire Henry, at least, are firm friends. As long, that is, as Henry respects the alphas in the pack and makes sure that he presents no challenge.

The first meeting between the vampire and the pack was in Holland during World War II, when Henry was working for the British Secret Service and the pack's grandfather, Perkin Heerkens, was with the Dutch Resistance. The pack, one of the last werewolf packs in Canada, have since become sheep farmers in Ontario, but now someone is killing them off, and it's up to Vicki and Henry to find out who and why.

Support group

In R. Chetwynd-Hayes delightful book *The Monster Club*, the supernatural creatures have banded together in the face of human hostility to form a sort of monster support group, and all get along fine; so much so that George Hardcastle, the werewolf, and Carola, the vampire, meet, fall in love, marry, and have the world's first werevamp!

In *Being Human*, werewolf George lives happily with vampire Mitchell, although in this series it's the wolves who are solitary creatures, while the vampires are organized and usually live in groups. The housemates support and help each other on a regular basis—George and Mitchell even work together. They are good friends, and not just because they're both outcasts. But they seem to be the exceptions.

Outside of the cosy home Mitchell, George, and Annie have created, we discover that vampires and werewolves are enemies. The vampires other than Mitchell in the series are shown as being vicious, ruthless, and thoroughly nasty, without a shred of humanity left: they torment George and it's obvious they look down on werewolves, calling them "doggies." This is possibly because when in human form, werewolves are very much weaker than vampires and therefore easy prey, and it's in the nature of the vampires in this series to abuse anyone or anything weaker than themselves, which of course includes humans.

The contrast between Mitchell, struggling so hard to hold onto the last shreds of his humanity, and the rest of the vampires who have given themselves over to the darker side of power, makes them appear even worse.

ENCOUNTERS WITH WEREWOLVES

So, in general, when a vampire encounters a werewolf, bloodshed is the result. But why? It's understandable in the *Underworld* movie trilogy, given that the vampires have enslaved and mistreated werewolves since the creatures were first created, but outside that the enmity seems, on the face of it, a little odd.

Werewolves and vampires are two different species, with different physiologies and feeding habits, and by rights shouldn't need to encounter each other, except perhaps on full-Moon nights when both are out hunting. Although even then they target different prey.

Loss of control

Maybe it's the werewolves' loss of control that is the root of the hostility. When werewolves transform, the wolf takes over, the higher functions are lost, and anything in its path is seen as food or something to be destroyed. For a species as fastidious as the modern vampire, such loss of control is something to be feared. Not only is it unseemly, but it can be dangerous, as the results can alert humans to the existence of a threat in their midst and then no one is safe. It also reminds the vampire that he, too, is capable of such loss of control—something he would probably prefer to forget.

Jealousy?

Perhaps there's a measure of jealousy in the interaction. Werewolves aren't immortal. In fact, given the huge and agonizing stresses to which their bodies are subject every month of every year

WORKING AT BEING HUMAN

Tortured vampire Mitchell, from the UK TV series *Being Human*. Torn between his near-overwhelming need for blood and his desperate desire to be human, Mitchell agonizes quietly over his choices, determined that he shouldn't let his friends suffer on his account.

of their entire life, they may very well not live as long as an equivalent fully human individual. They yearn to be human again; to not have to live under such a curse.

No worries

Vampires, on the other hand, suffer once, when first turned, and afterward are immortal and near-indestructible. They don't have the usual daily worries of the werewolf, after all, the human half has to eat, work, live among humans as one of them. In strict survival terms, the vampire's life is less stressful that the werewolf's.

From the vampire's point of view, the werewolf doesn't have the problems of coping with a nocturnal life and having to avoid the Sun. He can enjoy all the things that humans enjoy: the taste of food, the warmth of Sun on the skin, and the colors of daylight. But perhaps, in the final analysis, it's simply a natural antipathy, something innate that leads them to hate each other, the mistrust and distaste of one supreme predator for another. We may never know...

UNDERWORLD

The vicious hostility between vampires and werewolves is never so clearly demonstrated than in 2003's *Underworld*. Then again, given the way the vampires have treated the werewolves from the time of their creation, perhaps this isn't so surprising...

Vampires on TV

The vampire has a thoroughly enduring appeal and it has cropped up in an enormous number of popular TV series and made guest appearances in almost every major genre.

POPULAR APPEAL
However, there are also a large number of TV shows that focus primarily on the vampire and his place in the world.

Animated vampires
Premiered in 1990, *Gravedale High* was a 13-episode cartoon by Hanna-Barbera and NBC Productions. Rick Moranis voiced Max Schneider, a human who had unwittingly taken a job as a teacher at Gravedale High, a school specifically for monsters. The student body included Vinnie Stoker, Fonzie-esque vampire in quiff, jeans and leather jacket; nerdy werewolf Reggie

Seen-on-TV characters
Here is a list of all the vampires you may come across on the small screen:

➔ *Count Von Count, the counting vampire muppet in* Sesame Street *hit TV screens in the early 1970s.*

➔ *1977 saw the rather silly* Hardy Boys *and* Nancy Drew Meet Dracula *(Season Two, Episode One).*

➔ Starsky and Hutch *had a brush with* The Vampire *(Season Two, Episode Five, 1976).*

➔ The Quantum Leap *Season Five, Episode* Blood Moon *(1993) had a vampire theme.*

➔ *The Jeremy Brett* Sherlock Holmes *series tackled* The Last Vampyre *(1993, based on the Holmes story* The Case of the Sussex Vampire*).*

➔ *Dr. Jack Stewart accepts a date with a possible vampire in* Diagnosis Murder *(Season Two, Episode Thirteen, 1995: The Bela Lugosi Blues).*

➔ The X-Files *dealt with vampires twice (Season Two, Episode Seven, 1994) and* Bad Blood *(Season Five, Episode Twelve, 1998).*

➔ Relic Hunter *also had two vampire-related episodes,* Possessed *(Season One, Episode Twenty, 2000) and* Vampire's Kiss *(Season Three, Episode Seven, 2001).*

➔ Smallville *visited the vampire in* Thirst *(Season Five, Episode Five, 2005).*

➔ *2006 saw* Blade: the Series, *a twelve-part show based on the adventures of the vampire-hunting dhampir Blade.*

Moonshroud; the tiny and obnoxious Frankentyke; Gill Waterman, lagoon creature and surfer dude; Cleofatra, an obese bandage-wrapped mummy; Blanche the Southern belle zombie; and Duzer, a Valley girl whose hair was a mass of snakes like Medusa. Lightweight but very amusing, the show provided an insight into the problems of teenage monsters!

JAPANESE VAMPIRES

The vampire has made an appearance in Japanese Anime (the animated stories, similar to Western cartoons but considerably more elaborate and taken far more seriously) and Manga (comics and graphic novels), as well.

Vampire Princess Miyu

Made in 1989, *Vampire Princess Miyu*, is perhaps the earliest well-known series. Miyu appears to be around 14 years old, but is in fact a great deal older. She can only drink blood from those who give it willingly.

A dhampir

One of her parents was human, the other a vampire, making her a dhampir and hunter of demons: in this case "shinma" (god-demons), enormously powerful creatures from the demon realm who prey on humans. She is aided by Larva, a Western shinma, whose blood awakened her vampire side when she drank from him against his will.

Vampire Knight

Yuki Cross features in *Vampire Knight*. As the prefect of Cross Academy, an exclusive boarding school for vampires learning to coexist with humans, Yuki's life was once saved by a vampire as another attacked her.

Trinity Blood

Trinity Blood is a massively detailed and complex continuum. When humans try to colonize Mars in an attempt to deal with a population explosion, they discover the nanomachines, the Bacillus, which turn humans into vampires needing blood to survive.

This leads to a horrific war from which, 900 years later, the humans are still trying to recover. Vampires, known as Methuselahs, the Long-Lived Race, coexist uneasily with the humans: the Vatican acts as arbitrator in keeping the peace between the two sides.

Also in the equation are the Crusniks, immensely powerful creatures created from the Crusnik nanomachines—vampires who drink the blood of other vampires. The name was probably inspired by the Slovenian vampire, the Kresnik.

Much of the start of the Anime concerns the exploits of Abel Nightroad, a Crusnik who appears superficially to be an ever-hungry priest, bad with money, who is sent out on peace-

THE MUNSTERS ↑

Just your ordinary everyday American family-next-door... Lily Munster and Grandpa were the vampires in the family, but the rest of them weren't exactly normal either—except for Lily's sister Marilyn, the embarrassingly human one. They suffered all the trials and tribulations of a normal working family.

THE ADDAMS FAMILY →

The distinctly more upper-class counterparts to the Munsters. The Addams family weren't obviously monstrous, but they did have some odd and unsettling characteristics. Independently wealthy and with no need to conform, they were serenely unaware of the fear they inspired in others.

keeping missions by the Vatican; missions which usually end with him having to call on his powers to fight.

MUNSTERS AND ADDAMS

The Munsters and *The Addams Family* were two series that were similar in concept, but quite different in style. *The Munsters* ran for 70 episodes between 1964 and 1966, while *The Addams Family* ran for 64 episodes during the same time.

Munster mash

Despite being monsters, the Munsters are portrayed as an average working family. Herman Munster, who looks very like Boris Karloff's version of Frankenstein's monster, is the hard-working father. His wife, Lily, is a vampire, as is Grandpa. Herman and Lily's son, Eddie, is a werewolf. The other member of the family, the "black sheep," is Marilyn, Lily's sister, who is a perfectly normal human.

Addams family

The Addams Family, on the other hand, are very wealthy and aristocratic, and while they do look as though they ought to be monsters, they are really just very unusual humans. Or so we are led to believe.

Gomez Addams owns several companies and has stocks in many more, though he is very vague about money and often child-like in his general demeanor. He adores his graceful, refined wife, Morticia, a statuesque woman of vampiric appearance.

The Addams kids

They have two children; the sweet girl Wednesday and the inventive boy Pugsley. Uncle Fester (Gomez's brother), Morticia's Grandmama the witch, Lurch the butler, and Thing, the useful disembodied hand, makes up the rest of the eccentric household. The family members have vague and usually unspecified magical abilities such as Morticia being able to light candles from a distance.

There is a bit of a hiatus in vampire shows after *Dark Shadows*, mostly filled by vampire-biased episodes of other popular TV programs, but then came *Buffy the Vampire Slayer*.

BUFFY THE VAMPIRE SLAYER

First released as a film in 1992, starring Kristy Swanson as Buffy, the film was played as a comedy-horror hybrid. Buffy Summers is a popular, if air-headed, cheerleader in an LA school. Her main concerns are clothes and shopping with her friends, until she is approached one day by Merrick Jamison-Smythe, who tells

---

BUFFY AND THE SCOOBY GANG

The latest in a long line of vampire slayers, over the years of the long-running series Buffy gathered together a dedicated group of friends and helpers, who became known as the Scooby Gang, after the ghost-hunting group of teenagers in the Scooby-do cartoons.

her that she is a Vampire Slayer and he is her Watcher, sent to guide and train her.

Guidance and training

Her response to this is, predictably, outright disbelief and mockery. However, he persists, and given the impetus of her lucid and frightening dreams of a past self, Buffy finally gives in and starts training. She realizes how serious things are when Merrick is killed by the Master Vampire Lothos, and everything comes to a head when the vampires attack the senior prom.

The writer

Joss Whedon, the writer, was unhappy with the movie. He'd wanted to portray Buffy as an empowered, independent, strong woman, with the film having an altogether darker tone. He was tired of the "little blonde girl goes into a dark alley and is killed by monsters" theme of many previous works; he wanted the young blonde to fight back, to become a heroine.

The character and general concept that Whedon had originally aimed for caught the popular imagination with the long-running TV series, first aired 10 March 1997.

Moving to California

The TV show starred Sarah Michelle Gellar as Buffy. After the events in the 1992 film, Buffy and her mother move to Sunnydale, California, to regain some control over their lives.

However, it transpires that the library of Sunnydale High, Buffy's new school, is actually situated over a Hellmouth, a portal to the demon realms that allows all manner of supernatural threats to emerge. Guided by her new Watcher, Rupert Giles, and assisted by a loyal band of friends known as the Scooby Gang, or Scoobies, Buffy battles an increasingly varied and powerful assortment of vampires, demons, and monsters throughout the seven seasons of the show.

Villain of the week

Each episode had a "villain of the week" as well as being part of a much larger plot arc, and often also had a major villain, the story of which usually spread over a whole season. In Season One this was The Master, an ancient and exceptionally evil vampire.

Angel appears in the second season, and goes on to star in his own, very successful, series. The Scoobies all develop over the course of the whole show, becoming powerful warriors in their own right, while a number of the bad guys switch sides—the vampire Spike among them.

Major impact

All in all, the series had a major, mainly positive, impact on the younger TV-watching public, especially in its depiction of strong, independent, and self-determining female characters, and generated a solid ongoing fanbase.

It also portrayed vampires as capable of acting for good rather than evil; still a fairly novel concept at the time, but one which alleviated the unease some people felt about finding vampires attractive.

Angel

The much darker-toned Angel was a very successful, occasionally even more successful than its parent, spin-off from *Buffy*. The character of Angel, the vampire whose soul is restored and who then spends his nights trying to make restitution for all the evil he has done in the past, proved immensely attractive to the viewing public. The series went on for five seasons.

Private detective

Like Buffy, Angel assembles a band of loyal followers and partners in his private detective agency Angel Investigations, including an Irish half-demon and the green-skinned, horned, pacifist demon Lorne.

Again, like *Buffy*, each episode has a villain, and the evil law firm of Wolfram and Hart are the ongoing bad guys of the series. Angel himself is portrayed with sympathy, and his struggles to stay true to his ideals are handled well.

TRUE BLOOD

Set in the fictional town of Bon Temps, Louisiana, in the near future, the television series *True Blood* is based on the *Sookie Stackhouse* books by Charlaine Harris. The basic premise is the Japanese invention, *TruBlood*, which allows vampires to stop feeding on humans and come out of the coffin, so to speak, hopefully soon to take their place as equals with the human race.

The fight for emanicpation

That's the theory, anyway. In reality, the mainstream world is a little less enthusiastic about welcoming vampires into the community and they are portrayed as a victimized minority. There is even a tiny glimpse of a billboard displaying "God Hates Fangs" (echoing the Westboro Baptist Church's "God Hates Fags" slogan) in the opening credits.

And here in backwoods Louisiana, down in the Deep South, where the pace of life changes slowly, if at all, vampires face an almost insuperable uphill struggle.

The power of blood

They face other challenges, too. Their blood, it has been discovered, has a wonderfully healing and rejuvenating effect on human physiology, acting like a drug, and like any drug, there are those who become addicted and go to any lengths to obtain it. Referred to as "V-juice," a thriving black market develops in trading the commodity.

The plot begins two years after the vampire community has "come out." Barmaid Sookie Stackhouse saves vampire Bill Compton from an attack in a diner parking lot when some thugs try to steal Compton's "V-juice" blood.

Love triangle

Though Sookie falls for Compton early on in the series, diner owner Sam Merlotte completes the love triangle. In a world where girls who fraternize with vampires are often derided as "fang bangers," sometimes even murdered, the series mixes social comment and fantasy with a dark, twisted humor.

Vampires in Literature

GUEST APPEARANCES

The vampire has made a guest appearance in almost every major genre in literature. Even Sherlock Holmes once had an encounter with one in *The Adventure of the Sussex Vampire,* although of course, this being the ultra-rational Holmes, the vampire eventually turns out to be something else entirely.

Harry Potter

Vampires are mentioned throughout the J.K. Rowling *Harry Potter* books, but more as a natural part of the magical world than as significant characters. Many people in the wizarding world fear them. The Ministry of Magic seems to consider them to be non-wizard part-humans, and they're studied as part of the Defence Against the Dark Arts classes.

NOTABLE VAMPIRE APPEARANCES

The following are just a few of the more well-known books out of the wide variety of vampire stories available.

Varney the Vampire

By James Malcolm Rhymer, *Varney the Vampire* was the original "penny dreadful"; an epic tale selling for a penny per chapter, each chapter finishing on a cliffhanger so that the reader would feel compelled to buy the next instalment to find out what happened next.

Varney the Vampire or *The Feast of Blood* was a truly mammoth work, finishing up lasting for 868 pages of script divided into 220 chapters. The basic story concerns the Bannerworth family and the troubles that Sir Francis Varney, the vampire, inflicts upon them. During the course of the story, Varney gradually changes from being an evil monster into a more sympathetic character. He's shown as loathing his condition, and eventually commits suicide by throwing himself into the volcano Mount Vesuvius, Italy.

Physical appearance

Varney's appearance is quite alarming, but accurate as a description of the more traditional vampire, and many of his features, both physical and behavioral, became standard in later vampire fiction.

He is also able to endure sunlight and possesses superhuman strength and hypnotic powers.

VARNEY THE VAMPIRE

Varney the Vampire or *The Feast of Blood.* Sir Francis Varney, a vampire of the most loathsome appearance and habits, targets the Bannerworth family to slake his unholy thirsts.

No. 1.]　　Nos. 2, 3 and 4 are Presented, Gratis, with this No.　　[Price 1d.

VARNEY THE VAMPIRE.

OR THE

FEAST OF BLOOD

A ROMANCE OF EXCITING INTEREST.

BY THE AUTHOR OF
"GRACE RIVERS; OR, THE MERCHANT'S DAUGHTER."

LONDON: E. LLOYD, SALISBURY-SQUARE, AND ALL BOOKSELLERS.

Unlike most later vampires, he is able to eat and drink normal food, but it didn't really agree with him. The story sold between 1845 and 1847, and in 1847 was published in single-volume form.

I AM LEGEND

In 1954 Richard Matheson's seminal novel *I Am Legend* was released. It tells the story of Robert Neville, seemingly the last human left alive after a global virus, with symptoms that resemble vampirism, infects the rest of the human species.

The story covers the period between 1975 and 1978. It chronicles Neville's descent into depression and drinking, and later his attempts to research and find a cure for the disease. Every night he has to defend himself from the attacks of the vampires, who attempt to entice him out. He discovers that the disease is caused by bacteria that inflicts vampirism on both the living (the infected) and the dead (true vampires).

Biological anomaly

Neville finds an apparently uninfected woman, Ruth, and brings her into his home. In fact she is infected, and takes him captive. Ruth explains that the infected are adapting, learning how to endure short spells of sunlight, and learning to deal with the condition. They have no choice, after all; they can't cure it and are beginning to build a new way of life adapted to the limitations of the disease.

Neville, in fact, is now the biological anomaly in a new world. The infected, the new rulers of the Earth, are gradually destroying the dangerous, true vampires, but there is no place for Neville in this new stage of human evolution, and as he has been murdering living people the others want him dead.

Three films

The story was adapted into three different films over the years: *The Last Man on Earth* in 1964, starring Vincent Price; *The Omega Man* in 1971, starring Charlton Heston; and the 2007 Will Smith vehicle *I Am Legend*. None of them is completely true to the novel, but the third is the furthest removed, changing the end completely, to the detriment of the story.

THE HUNGER

The 1981 book *The Hunger* by Whitley Strieber presents vampires as a completely separate species of being from humans, but living among them unnoticed, not quite immortal, but unchanging once they reach maturity.

Beautiful vampire Miriam Blaylock, whose life dates back to Ancient Egyptian times, has discovered that a transfusion of her blood will grant prolonged life and youth to her chosen human, but only for a certain period of time, after which they age rapidly. The horror is that they do not and cannot die, even though they become nothing more than a withered husk. Miriam has been following the work of a young physician, Dr. Sarah Roberts, in the hope that it might provide a cure for the problem of the sudden rapid aging in her lover, John. When he becomes uncontrollable, she turns her attentions to Sarah instead.

Top 10 fiction female vampires

Nice or nasty, or perhaps a little of each, this colorful selection of female vampire characters are the very best of the bunch:

→ **Selene the Death Dealer**, powerful, dedicated, and independent.

→ **Carmilla**, an intriguing mix of passion and despair, lust and love, whose infatuation with Laura led to her own downfall.

→ **Vampirella**, the beautiful, voluptuous, and scantily-clad blood drinker from the planet Drakulon, who came to Earth to save her dying people. Once here, she turned her hand to good, fighting with the demon hunter Adam van Helsing to protect the human race.

→ **Claudia**, created by Louis and Lestat, demonic child-vampire whose cruelty exceeded even Lestat's. Tortured by adult feelings frustrated by a body that would never grow past childhood, her death came as a welcome release.

→ **Saya**, of the Japanese Anime, Manga comics and 2009 live-action film Blood, the Last Vampire, is the last of her kind, and fights the deadly chiropterans—immensely long-lived, highly intelligent creatures that live on human blood—with a katana and her supernatural strength and speed.

→ **Lucy Westenra**, Dracula's first British victim. Although it could be argued she wasn't a strong enough character to make a really good vampire...

→ **Akasha**, Mother Vampire and a thoroughly nasty character, although her plan to kill off 90 percent of the male population of Earth and keep the best for breeding purposes is an interesting take on dreams of global domination, and one that could appeal to a lot of women. However, her desire to be worshiped as a goddess perhaps isn't such a good idea.

→ **Darla**, the late-16th-century vampire who in 1753 turned Liam, later to become Angel, afterward keeping him as her consort. She used her beauty to lure her prey, rather than hunting.

→ **Quintana**, the beautiful vampire with the V-SAN organization in Bloodsuckers (aka Vampire Wars). A telepath as well as having the traditional speed and strength of the vampire, she is initially deeply disliked by her coworkers, but she finally convinces them she is on their side and becomes a valued team-member.

→ **Freda Sackville-Bagg**, mother to the Little Vampire Randolph. Beautiful, elegant, and refined, she charms rather than seduces everyone she meets.

IMMORTAL BLOOD

Immortal Blood (aka *Those Who Hunt by Night*), is the 1989 vampire novel by the prolific and popular Barbara Hambly. At the beginning of the 20th century Don Simon Xavier Christian Morado de la Cadena-Ysidro, Ysidro for short, the oldest of the vampires of London, contacts James Asher, formerly of Her Majesty's Secret Service.

Ysidro requests the help of Asher, now a professor of history and linguistics at Oxford University, to uncover the identity of whoever is killing vampires. Asher is reluctant, but Ysidro threatens his wife Lydia, a talented physician, to compel his compliance.

Strong mental powers

The vampires possess the traditional characteristics, burn in the Sun, and have supernatural strength and speed, but they are also shown as having particularly strong mental powers, able to "blank" human minds and memories so as to pass unseen. They are also allergic to silver: while wearing the metal doesn't stop a vampire's attack, it does make it more difficult. Asher believes that, given the strength and general invulnerability of vampires, the killer must be a vampire himself, but one who can endure sunlight. He enlists Lydia's help, and as he searches the crypts and cellars of London, she hunts down medical and property records, looking for clues.

SAINT-GERMAIN STORIES

Chelsea Quinn Yarbro started writing the Saint-Germain stories with *Hotel Transylvania* in 1978, although it's not chronologically the first book in the series.

Her vampire, Franciscus Ragoczy Saint-Germain, or variations thereof, was inspired by the mysterious Comte de Saint-Germain, who was a genuine historical person, although not much is known about him. He was a scientist and alchemist of the time, the 18th century, but let it be known that he had lived for several centuries, and it was claimed that he was of noble birth.

It's said that the Theosophists, whose philosophy was that all religions should help humanity, evolve toward perfection and a higher spirituality, considered him to be an immortal with almost god-like powers.

A prince

Yarbro's vampire is the son of the leader of his tribe, hence a prince in his own right, born around 1,500 years BCE in the area that would later become Transylvania. He is given over to the god of his tribe, a vampire, who is the one who turned him. But he is captured and sold into slavery when his tribe is attacked, and spends much of his early years in Ancient Egypt, learning the healing arts. Afterward he travels extensively, in part to hide the fact that he never ages. He uses his alchemical skills to transmute base metals into gold, but more unusually to create precious stones such as diamonds. He then uses these to provide for his needs, those of his friends, and those to whom he acts as patron—often women of unusual skills and talents whose gifts would otherwise be wasted.

"Oh God," he said softly, in his private torment. "You are willing, but you do not know what may happen to you. Can't you see that my very desire makes me dangerous to you?" He had taken her by the arms and was shaking her tenderly. "Madeleine, I burn for you, but I cannot. I cannot."

Hotel Transylvania

In later years he uses his wealth to invest in forward-looking businesses, such as avionics, which leave him able to live very comfortably and free to enjoy his interests.

A noble vampire

Saint-Germain is a noble vampire, ancient, wise, and compassionate. He casts no reflection, but can endure sunlight and running water by lining the soles of his shoes with his native earth, which he also mixes into the foundations of his homes.

A change in height

Yarbro is one of only a very few authors who have taken into account the fact that the human body has changed significantly in height over the centuries; we have all grown taller as a result of better nutrition and healthcare: Saint-Germain was taller than average when he was first turned, and is still considered tall in Roman times, but these days he is short for a man. Huff has also

touched on the subject: Henry Fitzroy is somewhat shorter than the average man, although 450 years ago he would have been fairly tall.

Tiny amounts

The most significant difference between Saint-Germain and most other vampires is that he needs only a very tiny amount of blood to live. He takes it either from his current lover or from a sleeping but willing victim, whose dreams he enters to give them ecstasy while he very gently feeds. It's the life energy he drinks while feeding that sustains him as much as the blood, and the trust and love he receives from his lovers is more important than the liquid itself.

Saint-Germain has existed through the millennia, traveling from one country to another, immersing himself in the culture, and often lending his vast knowledge and wisdom to the rulers.

Each story is meticulously researched and so it's quite possible to learn a considerable amount of history from these novels. Saint-Germain himself is a fascinating and compelling creature and his stories are some of the most interesting and memorable in vampire literature.

DETECTIVE FICTION

Detective fiction readily lends itself to the vampire genre. Having a partner who's bulletproof can hypnotize people to gain information, and has enhanced senses and strength, would make for a very strong crime-fighting duo. And that is just what P.N. Elrod has done in the *Vampire Files* series.

These tell the story of one of the first vampire detectives, Jack Fleming, an erstwhile New York newspaper reporter, wannabe novelist, and partner to private detective Charles Escott. The story is set in Chicago during the 1930s.

Jack wakes up on a beach, with no memory of how he got there. Someone tries to run him down, and he finds he's a lot stronger than he should be and has the ability to force people mentally to tell him the truth. He "persuades" the motorist to explain what's happened, and finds out that he was tortured and killed to find the location of a list that the gangsters wanted. But this doesn't help Jack very much, since he can't remember what the list is, or why it's important.

Finding out

By trial and error he slowly discovers what he is, and is horrified, as the thought of feeding on human blood is completely loathsome. However, he finds he is perfectly able to survive on the blood from the cattle at the Chicago stockyards and the cows can easily afford to spare the pint or two that he needs.

Finally Escott, whose curiosity has been aroused by Jack's activities and has been tailing him, confronts Jack with a cross, which has no effect on him, and on finding him both wronged and clueless, offers to help in return for Jack's assistance with a difficult case; or two.

A productive partnership

The partnership proves very productive, and even after Jack's memory has come back, in

excruciatingly painful fits and starts, the two continue to work together. Escott helps Jack start the search for Maureen Dupont, the vampire who turned him and who is still the love of his life. In the meantime, Jack becomes involved with Bobbi Smythe, a beautiful songstress, who he eventually trusts enough to reveal his nature. Theirs is a relationship of mutual passion: Jack compares human blood and cattle blood to the difference between champagne and milk—the champagne is glorious, but you wouldn't want to live on it and milk is better as an ordinary sort of drink.

Passing like mist

As a vampire Jack has one of the more interesting traditional vampiric abilities—to be able to become insubstantial and pass like mist through tiny spaces. He's not fond of doing it, as he loses all senses and has difficulty figuring out where he is, but it comes in extremely handy in his and Escott's line of work. It also allows him a sort of flight, as in this form he can rise to a considerable height. However, water of any kind almost completely incapacitates him, making boat trips near-impossible and even crossing water a trial.

GUILTY PLEASURES

The language and tone of *Guilty Pleasures*, the first Laurell K. Hamilton, *Anita Blake, Vampire Hunter,* has echoes of Philip Marlowe and Sam Spade, the great fictional American private investigators. The basic story: that something is killing vampires, who call in a professional to deal with the killer, isn't new. In *Guilty Pleasures* the city's Master Vampire wants Anita Blake, zombie animator and vampire killer, to handle the case, and threatens friends and coworkers to make sure she complies. Apparently Anita is the best there is. She's more than competent with all types of physical weaponry, especially guns, and is trained in several martial arts; all very useful in her side-line of licensed vampire hunter, usually employed to hunt down and kill vampires that have killed humans. She's also an agent on retainer with the local chapter of the Regional Preternatural Investigation Taskforce (known as Rip-it), the agency tasked with solving supernatural crimes. Anita is also a devout Christian, which leads to soul-searching about her religious beliefs and what she does for a living.

Personality problems

As a person she's not particularly likeable. Her constant whingeing about how scared, fearful, and terrified she is becomes wearying after a while (it feels as though it's mentioned at least once every other page), and she's a self-confessed trouble magnet who only brings danger to her friends, yet still insists on involving them in her cases. She also seems to acquire new abilities in each story, making her more and more powerful and running the risk of being seen as a Mary Sue.

Vampire glamor

Blake's vampires are incredibly beautiful at first sight, but it seems this is something of a glamor they use to hide perceived imperfections from human eyes, and to help them attract their victims. Anita has been targeted by the Master Vampire Jean-Claude, who has marked her as his own, with a view to eventually making her his human servant.

Old vampires

The old vampires in these books are extremely powerful: New Orleans' Master Vampire is at least a thousand years old, can take over anyone's mind without a second thought, and can "fly." She also looks like a little girl (even though her name is Nikolaos). Ability-wise, the vampires have a lot in common with the Volturi of the *Twilight* series, although they seem much less interested in protecting their own kind.

VAMPIRE EQUALITY

While in the Anita Blake books the vampires already have legal recognition and equal rights, in the Sookie Stackhouse novels, laws are going through the legal system to recognize vampire equality with humans and to grant the vampires equal rights. Vampires do at least now have the legal right to exist. The Vampire Rights Amendment (the VRA) is a proposed amendment to the American Constitution ratification. There are just two simple but vital provisions: to give vampires equal rights under the law, and to grant Congress the right to enforce these rights. In the *Haadri Cycle*, the Nameless have the ultimate goal of coexisting with their mortal counterparts openly and safely, but accept that it will take a very long time before the mortal world will accept them.

Where do we go from here?

We've moved from the vampire as terrifying, demon-cursed corpse to the vampire as potentially desirable neighbor, from monster to near-equal. In a 24-hour non-stop world, it will be interesting to see where we go from here.

Women Vampire Writers

WHY WOMEN?

It's notable that the vast majority of vampire books, these days, are written by women. Why is this? There are a number of possible reasons.

DIFFERENCE BETWEEN THE SEXES

Generally, writers of women's books often emphasize the relationship side of life, right from Jane Austen up to today's vast bookshelf of chick-lit titles. The setting and action are less important than the people and the ways they relate to each other.

Is this because women are expected and raised to enjoy such concepts, or because there is some quality that girls are born with that makes them respond to them? Is it a matter of nurture or nature?

One answer might be that as it's women who carry the future, who give birth to the next generation. They have a vested interest in ensuring that any relationships they involve themselves in should be wholesome and trustworthy.

This doesn't always work in the real world. However, by reading and watching books and films that deal with fictional relationships of all kinds, women can learn second-hand how various relationships might play out.

FALLING SHORT

Another possibility is more logical. Even the most practical and sardonic of women, living with no illusions about men, may find their relationships with the opposite sex falling far short of their hopes and aspirations: for those who've been brought up to expect to be treated like a princess, or even as an equal, this can come as a real shock.

In such cases women may be obliged to look elsewhere, to a fantasy lover or a fantasy life, which is fine, of course, as long as it doesn't take over their real lives.

FANTASY LOVER

As we've seen in the course of this book, the vampire is an ideal fantasy lover. Dark, brooding, powerful, with an edge of danger, he is more than capable of sweeping his lover off her feet and into his perilous world, either with a view to keeping her safe or to allow her to join him in eternity.

However, women write about relationships, about fantasy lovers, as well as reading about them. It's a way to sculpt an ideal figure, a perfect love, to create exactly what the woman wants in a lover, to satisfy at least in part a longing for that ideal. It's empowering. And the things that are powerful in our minds make us more powerful in our bodies; in ourselves.

CRUDE ATTEMPTS

Those first attempts will probably be clumsy, as we learn the necessary skills to create what we perceive as perfection. But as we grow, develop, and refine the art, so too do our creations grow and develop, becoming real to us and figures of desire for others. They are no longer "perfect" creatures. Perfection is boring. We prefer our heroes to have a few flaws; it makes them more interesting and compelling.

While vampires are obviously a way of flirting with the imagery of death as something dangerous and seductive, the author's reasons for wishing to explore these themes may be far more necessary than romance.

WORKING THROUGH LOSS

Anne Rice, author of *The Vampire Chronicle* series, lost a six-year-old daughter to leukemia. Just three years after this tragic event, Rice completed the novel *Interview With the Vampire,* in which she explores the theme of the child who cannot grow up. Claudia, the little girl vampire, is frozen in time, and it's not difficult to see the author working through the very real loss by using this fictional device. Vampires, and the fantasy genres as a whole, often become the canvas on which writers and society project ideas that may seem too difficult to handle were they not sublimated into some other form.

EXPLORATION

With growing confidence we can explore the fictional worlds we have created, people them with other beings, and enlarge them until the time comes when we are able to set ourselves free to discover other realms, darker mysteries, and more intense lives. At that point we become, literally, capable of anything.

It's a truly liberating, life-changing experience. Much like the vampire himself.

Top Ten Female Authors

This is a list of the top women authors who write about vampires:

➔ *Chelsea Quinn Yarbro.*

➔ *Freda Warrington.*

➔ *Tanya Huff.*

➔ *Anne Rice.*

➔ *Poppy Z. Brite.*

➔ *Nancy Collins.*

➔ *P.N. Elrod.*

➔ *Charlaine Harris.*

➔ *Stephenie Meyer.*

➔ *Laurell K. Hamilton*

The Vampire in Movies

INFLUENCES

In the late 20th and early 21st centuries, much of our perception of vampires comes from what we see on our movie and TV screens. It's perfectly understandable: it's a fast and easy way of taking in the information we need and the entertainment we want. No matter how much we may enjoy reading, it's a lot more immediate, quick, and easy to watch a documentary or a movie adaptation of a book than it is to read that book itself.

Pluses and minuses

There are advantages and disadvantages to this, of course. In watching a movie, the viewer has no choice but to see someone else's interpretation of the landscape, setting, tone, and the appearance and behavior of the characters, rather than envisioning them personally, as happens when you read a book. And reading the book after seeing the film is bound to color one's perception forever afterward.

Conveying subtleties

Then again, the medium of film can convey subtleties that the written word simply can't express succinctly or with any exactitude: the shy yet heated glances between lovers, the widening of eyes and the almost silent indrawn breath at the unexpected sight of the beloved... Sometimes movies also create new concepts that become part of the mythos. For example, while the vampires of previous legends preferred the night,

it was only in the 1922 silent film *Nosferatu* that a vampire was first shown being destroyed by sunlight. Due to the film's popularity, the concept quickly spread and it is now rare for a vampire *not* to be harmed by sunlight. Likewise, the idea that a vampire burnt to ashes could be revived by just a few drops of blood supposedly only came into being when the Hammer Horror studios wanted to make a sequel to their hugely successful 1958 *Dracula* film.

Adaptations

Naturally, some movie adaptations of the written story are more accurate than others, or more true to the spirit of the book; the two are not necessarily the same. What follows on the next few pages is a brief look at some of the more significant vampire movies that have been made during the last hundred years.

VAMPIRE IMPERIOUS →

Count Orlok at his commanding best, taking control of the ship carrying him—and his rats carrying the plague—to his new home in Wisborg. *Nosferatu* was the first film to portray the vampire as being destroyed by sunlight—an idea that swiftly took hold.

Dracula Movies

 This is a list of the best-known Dracula movies, from the very first one up to the present day.

Nosferatu
Released: 1922
Director: F.W. Murnau
Actors: Max Schreck as Graf Orlok

The first, and still highly effective, interpretation of the Dracula story.

Dracula
The story of the strangest passion the world has ever known.
Released: 1931
Director: Tod Browning
Actor: Bela Lugosi as Count Dracula

Lugosi played another vampire, Count Mora, in the 1933 film *Mark of the Vampire,* and the vampire Armand Tesla in *Return of the Vampire* (1944).

Dracula (Horror of Dracula)
Don't Dare See It...Alone!
Released: 1958
Director: Terence Fisher
Actor: Christopher Lee as Count Dracula

Lee reprised his role as the Count in *Dracula, Prince of Darkness, Dracula Has Risen From the Grave, Taste the Blood of Dracula, Scars of Dracula*, and *The Satanic Rites of Dracula*, among others. He dies at the end of each movie to be given ever more ingenious methods of resurrection in the next!

Dracula
Throughout history he has filled the hearts of men with terror, and the hearts of women with desire.
Released: 1979
Director: John Badham
Actor: Frank Langella (title role)

The time frame is shifted to the 1920s and the storyline is quite different to Stoker's book. Nevertheless it's a seductive and compelling interpretation.

Dracula
Love Never Dies
Released: 1992
Director: Francis Ford Coppola
Actor: Gary Oldman (title role)
All-star, big-budget vampire love film. Sumptuous to look at, but a disappointment on a number of levels.

The **TERRIFYING** Lover – who died – yet lived!

Universal-International presents A Hammer Film Production

PETER CUSHING in

DRACULA

(Cert. **X**) Adults only

Also starring **MICHAEL GOUGH**
and **MELISSA STRIBLING**
with **CHRISTOPHER LEE** as Dracula

In Eastman Colour processed by Technicolor

Screenplay by JIMMY SANGSTER   Associate Producer ANTHONY NELSON-KEYS
Produced by ANTHONY HINDS   Directed by TERENCE FISHER
Executive Producer MICHAEL CARRERAS

Distributed by Rank Film Distributors Ltd.

DON'T DARE SEE IT ALONE!

CHRISTOPHER LEE

A noble savage of a different kind! Christopher Lee's Dracula was aristocratic and compelling, but ruthless in his pursuit of his prey and impossible to disobey once he had chosen you as his next meal.

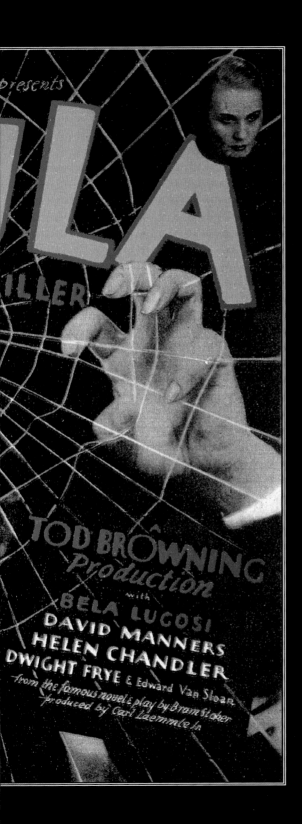

THE TANGLED WEB

Bela Lugosi in the 1931 version of *Dracula*. This movie poster accurately reflects the web of fear and desire that he wove around his victims. The movie showed the Count as suave and handsome, sure to thrill the female audience of the time.

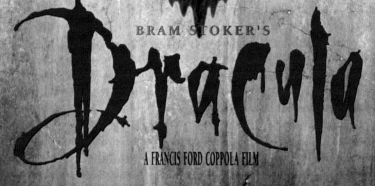

LOVE NEVER DIES

BRAM STOKER'S

Dracula

A FRANCIS FORD COPPOLA FILM

COLUMBIA PICTURES PRESENTS
AN AMERICAN ZOETROPE/OSIRIS FILMS PRODUCTION "BRAM STOKER'S DRACULA" GARY OLDMAN
WINONA RYDER ANTHONY HOPKINS KEANU REEVES PRODUCED BY JAMES V. HART VISUAL EFFECTS ROMAN COPPOLA
MUSIC BY WOJCIECH KILAR COSTUMES DESIGNED BY EIKO ISHIOKA EDITED BY NICHOLAS C. SMITH GLEN SCANTLEBURY ANNE GOURSAUD
PRODUCTION DESIGNED BY THOMAS SANDERS DIRECTOR OF PHOTOGRAPHY MICHAEL BALLHAUS A.S.C. EXECUTIVE MICHAEL APTED AND ROBERT O'CONNOR
SCREENPLAY BY JAMES V. HART PRODUCED BY FRANCIS FORD COPPOLA, FRED FUCHS AND CHARLES MULVEHILL
DIRECTED BY FRANCIS FORD COPPOLA

NOVEMBER

Vampire Movies

Vampire Circus
Released: 1972
Director: Robert Young
Actors: Adrienne Corri, Laurence Payne, Thorley Walters, John Moulder Brown, Elizabeth Seal, Lynne Frederick, Robine Hunter

Set in 1825, this horror-thriller comes across as being a little ridiculous, but it's pretty imaginative, too.

The vampire Count Mitterhaus preys on children. When the townsfolk revolt and storm his castle to kill him, with his dying breath he curses them and swears that their children will die to give him back his life.

Fifteen years later the area is being ravaged by the plague and no one is allowed to enter or leave it. Nevertheless the mysterious Circus of Night manages to pass the quarantine roadblocks and set up in the village square. The townsfolk, happy to have something to relieve the misery of their current existence, make them welcome.

But this is no ordinary circus. How is it that the trapeze artists are able to transform into owls at the peak of their swing? Is the naked dancer a human or a tigress? How is it that Emil can jump as a man yet land as a black panther? And what happens when people step through the mirror in the hall of mirrors?

The vampires are traditionally evil and vengeful, but the setting is unusual and the circus itself novel and mesmerizing.

FRANCIS FORD COPPOLA'S DRACULA, 1992

A love story spanning the centuries rather than a battle between good and evil as Stoker had intended, the film nevertheless stayed fairly close to the plot of the book. It was certainly an extravagant and lusciously designed movie.

Vampire Movies

Lifeforce

In outer space they unleashed a force more evil than the world had ever imagined.

Released: 1985
Director: Tobe Hooper
Genre: Sci-fi Horror

Based (very) loosely on Colin Wilson's novel *The Space Vampires*, *Lifeforce* is a distinct oddity in the realm of the vampire film.

A shuttle mission to investigate Halley's Comet finds an alien spacecraft hiding in the comet's head. The crew rescue and bring back to Earth three of the beings they find inside, two humanoid men and a beautiful humanoid woman.

Apparently dead on their arrival, the three beings later revive and the female escapes to cause chaos throughout London. They are psychic vampires, killing by draining the life-force of their victims, who later revive as a cross between psychic vampires and zombies themselves, draining life-force in their turn.

There's more to the female vampire than first appears, and the end is oddly touching.

The Lost Boys

Sleep all day. Party all night. Never grow old. Never die. It's fun to be a vampire.

Released: 1987
Director: Farhad Mann

After mother Lucy's divorce, the Emerson family move from Phoenix Arizona to Santa Carla, California, "Murder Capital of the World," as the welcome sign says, to live with her father while they get their life in order. There they become mixed up with the local vampire gang...

The teenage vampires, led by David, a splendidly threatening, brooding performance by Kiefer Sutherland, goad David into joining them, but his brother Sam, with the help of the vampire-hunting Frog brothers, isn't about to let that happen without a fight.

Near Dark

Released: 1987
Director: Kathryn Bigelow

Caleb Colton meets and falls for Mae, only to find out, too late, after she's bitten him, that she's a vampire. He joins her and the family in undeath, but proves to be a rather unsuccessful vampire as he refuses to kill.

Mae kills and allows him to feed from her, but this is hardly a satisfactory permanent solution. The resolution proves to be something of a surprise.

Near Dark is one of the grittier vampire films, realistic in its portrayal of the physical problems that the undead need to overcome in order to continue their existence.

Addams Family and Addams Family Values

Released: 1991 and 1993
Director: Barry Sonnenfeld

In the two main Addams Family films, *Addams Family* and *Addams Family Values*, the characters were changed a little, with Wednesday, superbly played by Christina Ricci, becoming a mature, dour child with a dry wit and a penchant for trying to kill her brother, while Pugsley is the slightly dim younger brother who tries to help Wednesday in her attempts to kill him. Raul Julia and Anjelica Huston are perfect as Gomez and Morticia, while Christopher Lloyd makes an excellent Uncle Fester.

From Dusk Till Dawn

Released: 1996
Director: Robert Rodriguez

Quentin Tarantino has acquired a well-deserved reputation for the graphic, if unrealistic, violence in his movies, so given that he wrote the screenplay, it's not surprising that it is a complete bloodbath.

Professional thief Seth Gecko and his psychopathic brother Richard are on the run from the FBI and the Texas police after killing three people, including a cop, in a liquor store hold-up. They take the Fuller family hostage, using their van to get themselves across the border into Mexico. They stop at a bar, the remote Titty Twister, and the Geckos insist on the Fullers having a drink with them before they're released. Unfortunately the bar is owned by, and full of, vampires. Mayhem ensues.

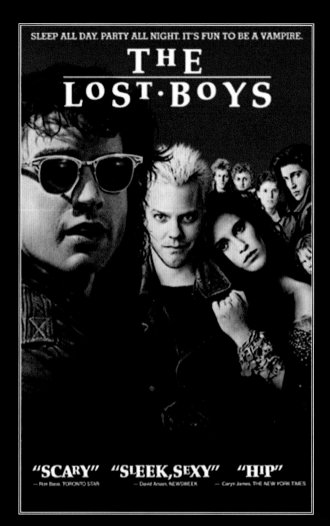

SLEEP ALL DAY. PARTY ALL NIGHT. IT'S FUN TO BE A VAMPIRE.

THE
LOST·BOYS

"SCARY"   "SLEEK, SEXY"   "HIP"
— Ron Base, TORONTO STAR   — David Ansen, NEWSWEEK   — Caryn James, THE NEW YORK TIMES

THE LOST BOYS

Jason Patric as bewildered and seduced newcomer
Michael, Kiefer Sutherland as fallen-angel-faced
David, the vampire leader of the Lost Boys, and the
lovely Jami Gertz as vampire-to-be Star. With this
movie vampires became the property of all ages of
fans, rather than the older generation's.

THE ADDAMS FAMILY

Starring Raul Julia as Gomez, the stunning Anjelica
Huston as Morticia, Christopher Lloyd as Uncle
Fester and Christina Ricci in one of her earliest roles
as Wednesday, this fun movie presented the
wonderfully dysfunctional family in a slightly more
serious vein than the pure comedy of the TV series.

Vampires Movies

Nick Knight
Released: 1998
Director: Farhad Mann

Something is killing people in Los Angeles, leaving their bodies drained of blood. Detective Nick Knight, who only ever works the night shift and doesn't have a partner, is assigned to the case.

Nick is a vampire who drives a '59 Cadillac because of its capacious trunk space—it being big enough for him to take refuge in if he's ever caught out in daylight.

He's recognized on the case by the archeologist Dr. Alyce Hunter, who has seen him in a very old photograph, and the two begin a tentative relationship, but his maker, LaCroix, is in town and not at all happy with Nick's ambitions.

Notable for being the movie that inspired the *Forever Knight* series, it's something of a curio now, and while the character of Nick Knight is sympathetic, especially in his struggle to become mortal again, the acting isn't wonderful and the ending is a something of a letdown.

Interview with the Vampire
Drink From Me And Live Forever.
Released: 1995
Director: Neil Jordan

In the latter half of the 20th century a young man sits in a spartan hotel room, tape recorder running on the table before him. Opposite him sits the vampire Louis de Pointe du Lac, revealing his life story into the machine...

As an exploration of what it means to be a vampire, with all the limitations and advantages, the hunger, loneliness, and alienation, as well as the struggle to survive in a world that could simply sweep one aside and move on, uncaring, it has yet to be bettered.

These are not nice people, but they are people, not stereotypes, with their own desires and motivations and unanswered questions. Fascinating and disturbing.

Blade

The power of an immortal. The soul of a human. The heart of a hero.
Released: 1998
Director: Stephen Norrington

Blade is a dhampir. He exists to hunt down and kill vampires; it's his sole purpose. But these vampires are organized, and a lot more dangerous than the vampires of legend. The elders; pure bloods, apparently born not made, which may argue for the ability of vampires in this continuum to reproduce physically, have existed in the shadows for centuries, running their affairs quietly and below the level of human perception.

Frost, who was made not born and thus is considered inferior by the elders, believes that vampires should be ruling the world and to this end has been researching vampire lore about La Magra, the vampire god who can bestow ultimate power.

Meanwhile, Dr. Karen Knight, who has been bitten by one of Frost's minions and is slowly turning, has been researching a way to reverse vampirism. She discovers that ethylenediaminetetraacetic acid (EDTA) reacts with vampire blood (and makes them explode rather messily).

In a typically ruthless display, Frost sacrifices the vampire elders to La Magra and gains the god's powers. Fortunately, before he can start enslaving the human race, Blade arrives and kills him with an overdose of EDTA.

Blade II

Know The Mark.
Released: 2002
Director: Guillermo del Toro

Two years after the events of the first movie, Blade is visited by two vampires asking for a truce in the face of a greater threat. A new creature has appeared, Nomak, infected with the Reaper virus, a hugely voracious strain of vampire that feeds viciously and daily on humans and vampires alike, making them Reapers in their turn.

The vampire elder Damaskinos requests that Blade lead the members of the Bloodpack, a group of vampires originally trained to hunt him down and kill him, temporarily until the Reaper threat is over.

It turns out, however, that the Reaper strain isn't a naturally evolving virus at all, and Blade has been betrayed.

Vampires Movies

Blade: Trinity
Released: 2004
Director: Len Wiseman

For the third outing, the vampires frame Blade for a human murder, resulting in his being wanted by the FBI.

In a seige, Blade's mentor is killed and Blade himself is captured, but freed shortly afterward by the Nightstalkers, a group of vampire hunters that includes Abigail, the daughter of Blade's first mentor and the smartass ex-vampire Hannibal King.

Meanwhile, one of the vampires, Dancia Talos, has located and resurrected the first and greatest vampire of them all, Dracula (known as Drake in the movie).

Talos hopes that Drake will strengthen the vampire species and kill Blade. However, the vampire hunters, the Nightstalkers, have developed the Daystar, a bioweapon that can kill all vampires in the area. The only problem is that it needs Drake's blood to become effective. As Drake is the first vampire his DNA is pure and would be the most effective. However the Daystar might kill the dhampir Blade along with the vampires.

Meanwhile, the vampires plan to take over the Earth and are working on what they call the "Final Solution." This film is not generally considered comparable to *Blade II*, the star of the trilogy, and it lacks the magic touch of director Guillermo del Toro. However, it has risen in popularity internationally since its release.

BLADE'S BLADES

Wesley Snipes as the dhampir vampire-hunter Blade, in the third movie of the trilogy. Grim, powerful, and relentlessly driven, Blade set the standard for vampire slayers to come.

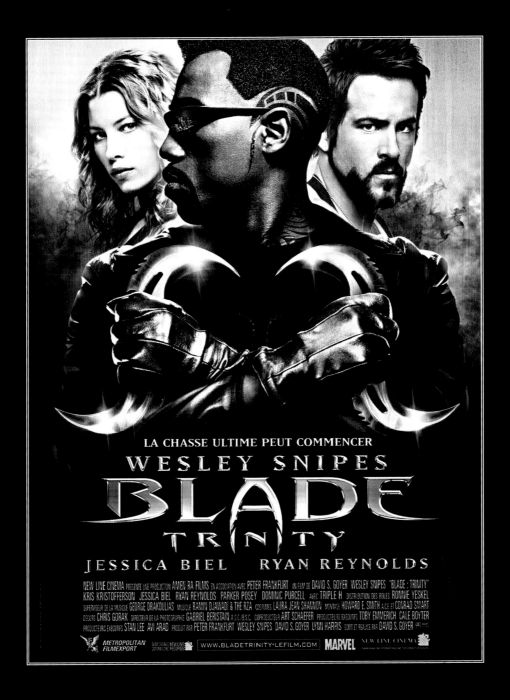

Vampires Movies

Underworld
Released: 2003
Director: Len Wiseman

Underworld: Evolution
Released: 2006
Director: Len Wiseman

Underworld: Rise of the Lycans
Released: 2009
Director: Patrick Tatopoulos

In the *Underworld* trilogy, the war between vampires and lycans (werewolves) has been going on for nearly a thousand years. The vampire Death Dealers believe they are close to wiping out the lycans for good.

The lycans, however, have been building up their numbers and developing effective and very nasty new weapons in hiding, to give them a chance to even the score.

And their leader, long thought to be dead, is in very secret, treacherous communication with the leader of the vampires.

Into the middle of this comes Michael Corvin, human, descendent of Alexander Corvinus, whose two sons were the original genetic vampire and werewolf.

The werewolves have somehow learned how to change without the Moon, so now have much more control of their animal natures.

30 Days of Night
They're Coming!
Released: 2007
Director: David Slade

Barrow, Alaska, a small town of around five hundred inhabitants, experiences a full month of perpetual darkness every year, when the Sun is below the horizon. Many of the townsfolk leave for warmer and brighter climes before this sub-zero winter, but a few remain to keep the essential services running: the town provides services for oil field operations.

As the last of the leavers head south for Fairbanks, those left find that all the cell phones have been destroyed, as have the town's dogs and the helicopter. A stranger is arrested for the crimes and incarcerated in the jail, raving that "They" are coming and everyone will soon be dead.

As the Sun sets for the last time for a month, the telecommunications center is attacked and disabled, cutting the town off from the outside world. Then the vampires attack, slaughtering most of the remaining inhabitants of Barrow.

This movie marks a return to the old traditional style of vampire: bestial, ruthless, and near-invincible, physically more animal than human. Impervious to the cold, incredibly fast, strong, and cunning, they are truly frightening creatures.

Although they obviously still possess their human intelligence, these vampires use a guttural language and the leader instructs the pack not to turn anyone so that the vampires will remain a myth to humans: when they have fed sufficiently they will burn the town and the bodies to destroy the evidence of their existence. They have lost any human emotion, and kill and feed indiscriminately. A powerful movie, and not one for those with weak stomachs.

The movie is based on a three-part horror comic of the same name by Steve Niles. In reality, Barrow is the northernmost settlement in the US. It has 67 days of night, and the temperature remains below freezing for most of the year. The average summer temperature is around eight degrees above freezing: perfect conditions for vampires.

Twilight

When you can live forever what do you live for?

Released: 2008
Director: Catherine Hardwicke

Seventeen-year-old Isabella Swan leaves her mother and hot, sunny Phoenix, Arizona, to live with her father for a while in cloudy, wet Forks on the Olympic Peninsula, Washington, USA.

Starting at the local school halfway through the semester, she's welcomed by most of the students, but finds herself drawn to the Cullens, a group of strange, ethereally beautiful people, and to Edward Cullen in particular.

They fall in love, but there's a problem. Edward Cullen is a vampire; one of a family who haven't fed on blood in decades, but being that close to a human is a very serious temptation.

30 DAYS OF NIGHT

BASED ON THE GRAPHIC NOVEL

OCTOBER
30DAYSOFNIGHT.com

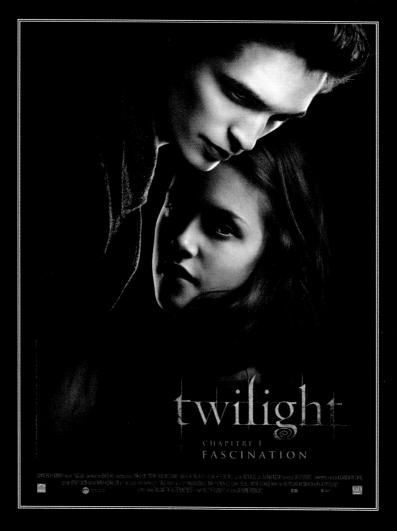

twilight
CHAPITRE I
FASCINATION

THE LONGEST MONTH

30 Days of Night is perhaps the most accurate portrayal of the traditional, folkloric vampire ever made. These vampires live as a pack: they are wholly amoral, driven only by the twin needs to survive and keep their existence secret. They kill indiscriminately, without mercy—they simply won't give up the hunt.

TWILIGHT

Robert Pattinson as the vampire Edward Cullen, with Kristen Stewart as his beloved Isabella Swan, from the first movie in the best-selling *Twilight* series. To know the love of a vampire is eternal bliss...

Twilight, the Movie

 When you can live forever what do you live for?

Set in the sublimely beautiful landscape of the Olympus Peninsula, Washington , *Twilight* (movie released in 2008) is the poignant story of a love that could last forever.

Isabella Swan is 17. Her parents are divorced and she lives with—and mostly looks after—her somewhat scatterbrained mother. Until, that is, her mother marries Phil Dwyer, a minor league baseball player, and wants to move with him to Florida. Although welcome to go with them, Bella opts to move to Forks, Washington, to spend time with her father and give her mom and Phil the opportunity to enjoy their new life together, by themselves. The difference between hot, sunny Phoenix, Arizona and wet, cloudy Forks comes as a shock to Bella, even though she is expecting it, but she's made her decision.

It's not as bad as it could be. Her father, Charlie, is a policeman in Forks, and while he obviously loves his daughter, like her he's not the affectionate, cuddly type and leaves her to settle in peace. Starting at the local school half way through the semester is never easy, but Isabella's made welcome by most of the students, who are a friendly, helpful bunch. For Bella, who had never really fitted in at her old

school, it's a surprise to find herself becoming popular, and not necessarily a pleasant one, as she lacks self-confidence, believing herself to be plain (which is untrue) and clumsy. And then she meets the Cullens.

She finds herself strangely drawn to this group of five ethereally beautiful people, and to Edward Cullen in particular. The problem is, he appears to loathe her, even going so far as to ask to change classes so he does not have to sit with her in science lessons. Bella can't understand his attitude, and feels unbalanced and a little distressed—a situation not helped by his sometimes seeming to like her and others not wanting to be near her. Then he saves her life, stopping a skidding car from slamming into her with his bare hands, and at that point she realizes that her previous suspicions—that there's something strange about the young man—are true.

Little by little things begin to add up. A trip to La Push with schoolmates and Jacob Black, son of a friend of her father's and a Quileute Indian, has Jacob telling her about the legends of the area, that his tribe claim their ancestry from wolves, and their enemies are the "cold ones," vampires—and that the tribe and the Cullens have a treaty not to encroach on each others' territory. Finally Bella confronts Edward, who confesses with an understated and wary delicacy that he is a vampire, but a "vegetarian," one who only drinks the blood of animals. He hasn't tasted human blood in decades, and that's why he's so reluctant to be with her. Her blood, her soul, calls to him, threatening to overwhelm his control, and he is so bound to her, the thought of accidentally hurting her is agony.

That knowledge sets both of them free to be themselves. Edward takes Bella to a high meadow, where he can lie in the Sun and show her how his skin glitters and shines—the real reason the family live here, where it's cloudy most of the time, so the humans can't see how alien they are. He shares his past with her, the long years of his life, how he was turned in 1918, at the point of death from the Spanish influenza that was devastating Chicago at the time, and how their little family has lived since, moving whenever the mortals around them notice they aren't aging. But most of all he shares with her how precious she has become to him, and how much he loves her.

The reactions of his family are mixed. Carlisle and Esmee, the "parents," are happy for him, as is "sister" Alice, but Rosalie takes a deep dislike to the human, which leads to some friction within the family, discord that isn't resolved until *New Moon* in the novels. However, the Cullens aren't the only vampires around, as Bella discovers when during a baseball match in a storm in the mountains—the only way the Cullens can cover the supersonic "crack" of their bats hitting the balls is by playing the game in a storm, when the sound blends in with the thunder—they are approached by three strangers. The three newcomers, Laurent, James, and the exotically beautiful Victoria, are a roving group who, we realize, are responsible for the killings that had been troubling the area recently. The exchange of pleasantries is strained but polite, as neither side wishes any overt hostilities; after all, Laurent's group are outnumbered, and really hadn't realized they were encroaching on Cullen territory. But as the vampire trio turn to leave a stray gust of wind blows Bella's scent to them...

James is a tracker, a vampire who hunts humans for the joy of the kill, and the next few frantic hours are spent with the Cullens trying desperately to lead him off the trail while Alice and Jasper drive Bella to what they hope is safety. Unfortunately their efforts aren't successful, and the confrontations that follow are violent and nearly deadly for Bella. But only nearly. Edward and the family arrive just in time.

A week or so later, back in Forks, Edward takes the still-recovering Bella to the prom, and there, in a setting of shimmering beauty and teenage awkwardness hovering on the edge of a vaster, more profound, world, she tells him of her desire and determination to become a vampire and spend eternity with him.

The Comic Side of Undeath

 The darker and more intense aspects of the vampire have received much attention, but there is also a lighter side. Some wonderful vampire comedies have been made. What follows are some of the best:

Dance of the Vampires

Who says vampires are no laughing matter?
Released: 1976
Director: Roman Polanski

Absent-minded Professor Abronsius and his dopey assistant, Alfred, are vampire hunters. In a remote Transylvanian village Alfred falls for the inn-keeper's daughter Sarah. However, she has been noticed and marked for prey by Count Krolock, who lives in a dark, ominous castle not far from the village.

The movie is a wonderfully realistic portrayal of an unspecified but apparently 18th-century Eastern European country. Count Krolock and his gay son are deliciously creepy, their castle appropriately dusty and labyrinthine, and the snowy landscape is beautiful. The vampires here are traditional, purely evil and a menace to be destroyed, although the professor and Alfred are definitely not the "experts" to call in to perform the task.

Love at First Bite

Released: 1979
Director: Stan Dragoti

Forced out of his Transylvanian castle (which has to be sold to pay back taxes), Dracula arrives in New York to seek a bride. Bemused and confused by 20th-century life in America, he stumbles through the city in pursuit of Cindy Sondheim, a top model convinced that shse is the reincarnation of Mina Harker, his lover from years ago. Unfortunately, her boyfriend, Dr. Jeffery Rosenberg, is a distant descendent of Abraham Van Helsing.

This Golden Globe-nominated comedy takes great joy in inverting the standard format. Dracula finds it near-impossible to get near his chosen victim, as the successful model is surrounded by security.

It takes tracking her down to her favorite club and a disco-dancing Dracula before he's in with a chance. Meanwhile Van Helsing, the would-be vampire hunter, is locked up for his "lunatic" behavior as he tries to dispatch the vampire.

Sundown: The Vampire in Retreat

There's two kinds of folks in Purgatory,
vampires and lunch.

Released: 1991

Director: Anthony Hickox

Mardulak, weary of being seen as a fiend and
desiring to see vampirekind live harmoniously
alongside humans, has bought the aptly
named Purgatory, a once-prosperous but
lately abandoned copper-mining town in the
Arizona desert, and gathered together a
community of vampires to live there.

At the same time, he hired Harrison to design
and build a plant for making synthesized
blood in the town, initially, of course, to
provide sustenance for the community, but in
the hope, shared by Harrison, that eventually
it would be able to cope with the human
demand for blood for transfusions.

The plant machinery has developed a fault,
however, slowing down production, and
Harrison, his wife, and their two little
daughters are asked to visit Purgatory to
correct the problem. Unfortunately, Shane,
one of the more recently turned vampires,
is an erstwhile friend of Harrison and turns
out to be an old lover of his wife's.

Add to that a Puritan member of the
community who does not believe in
Mardulak's vision and has been creating his
own army of vampires to force a return to the
old ways; the devising of hardened wooden
bullets that splinter when entering the body;
and the arrival of the bumbling but oddly
cute great-grandson of Abraham Van
Helsing, intent on carrying out his family's
destiny, and you have the perfect mix for one
of the more enjoyable and intelligent vampire
movies of the decade.

Sundown was probably the first movie to
present vampires as essentially being the
same as humans, with good and bad
individuals, and experiencing temptations,
goals, dreams, and desires comparable to
their living counterparts.

The Purgatory vampires are really nice
people, the sort you wouldn't mind having
for neighbors, although you might find their
need for blood a little alarming, as it's always
present, simmering below the surface.

The Comic Side of Undeath

Rockula

He's a vampire who hasn't scored in 400 years. Tonight's the night!

Released: 1990

Director: Luca Bercovici

Ralph LaVie is cursed. Four centuries ago he watched his one true love killed at Hallowe'en by a hambone-wielding pirate with a rhinestone pegleg, and he didn't stop it happening.

Ever since, he has had to watch his love be reincarnated every 22 years, over and over again, only to be killed over and over again in the same ghastly manner.

But now it's her nineteenth lifetime and he's had more than enough. THIS time Mona will finally be his...

Ralphie (as his mother calls him) is one of the strangest vampires ever. He can change into a bat, sort of, but he can't really fly.

He faints at the sight of fresh blood, and, as he sings in the title song, "If it wasn't for Red Cross donations this vampire would die." He's sweet and frustrated and loveable, and very human, despite his condition.

A musical, which includes bit parts for musicians Bo Diddley, Thomas Dolby, and Toni Basil, it's certainly an interesting attempt at mixing genres.

THE LEFT HAND OF GOD

Hugh Jackman stars as the brooding, heroic Gabriel Van Helsing, the monster-hunter employed by the Knights of the Holy Order. While the movie itself had huge plot holes, questionable logic, and some less than stellar acting, it's a good old-fashioned horror movie with its tongue stuck firmly in its cheek.

The Comic Side of Undeath

 ### The Little Vampire

They're not just best friends.
They're blood brothers.

Released: 2000
Director: Steven Sommers

Little Tony Thompson has had to move to Scotland with his parents while his father works on a major landscaping project for Lord McAshton. He hates it there: the schoolkids make fun of his American accent and he's bullied by McAshton's grandsons. He's also been having some very nasty nightmares about vampires.

And then he meets one, young Rudolph, and they become best friends. However, Rudolph and his family are being tracked by Rookery the vampire slayer, who wants to complete the job his ancestor failed to do three hundred years ago and kill them all.

This movie is for kids, with enough jokes aimed at the adults that the whole family can enjoy it. The tone tends toward "camp" rather than "scary," and of course the vampires feed only off cow blood throughout.

Nevertheless, the movie is thoroughly enjoyable and features some stellar performances from the whole cast, young and old. Notable parts include: Richard E. Grant as Frederick Sackvill-Bagg, head of the vampire family, and Jonathan Lipnicki of Stuart Little fame as human Tony Thompson.

Van Helsing

The one name they all fear...

Released: 2004
Director: Steven Sommers

Gabriel Van Helsing is a monster hunter for the Catholic Church, tasked to capture (preferably) or kill (if need be) the wide variety of fiends that haunt the world.

After disposing of Mr Hyde in Paris, he returns to base, only to be despatched to Transylvania to help the Valerious family destroy Dracula, so that the family will be able to go to Heaven.

Apparently an ancestor swore that none of them would rest in peace until the vampire was dead and since then none of them have.

Accompanied by the friar Carl, a 19th-century inventor, Van Helsing discovers that Anna is the last remaining member of the family, her brother having been recently turned into a werewolf, and after some argument they join forces to fight against the vampire.

Along the way they rescue Frankenstein's monster and kill off the myriad hatchling child vampires in the crypt; the result of Dracula having his three wives, it would seem, though the movie does not go into details about how this is done.

These vampires are of the traditional, pure-evil variety, treacherous, amoral, and malevolent. The females can change into half-human, half-bat hybrids, and Dracula himself transforms into an impressively demonic bat-like creature. They can all endure daylight, but only in cloudy weather: they hide from the Sun.

Bloodsuckers

Our whole existence depends on them.
Released: 2005
Director: Matthew Hastings

It's 2210 and the human race has been venturing out into the galaxy for a while now. Unfortunately they found that something else had got there first; an entire species of vampires of numerous different breeds, some of them friendly; the vast majority of them

not. To combat the vampire menace on those worlds where humanity has managed to gain a toehold, the V-SAN (Vampire Sanitation) unit was formed.

Bloodsuckers is the story of one of their missions. The V-SAN ship *Hieronymus* answers a distress call from a colony world and is immediately embroiled in combat with a particularly nasty bunch of vampires. The crew is assisted by the gorgeous vampire Quintana, whose psychic abilities are invaluable to their missions, but who is not particularly popular with the rest of the crew, some of whom don't believe she can be trusted.

There are several different clans of vampires shown in the movie, some of them intelligent and advanced, some of them little more than animals, but they are all prone to extreme violence and very untrustworthy.

Well worth watching, as long as you don't expect too much or anything the least bit high-brow.

Glossary

Amoral Without morals. Not necessarily evil or immoral, but unbothered about right and wrong; uncaring about moral judgments.

Baptism The ritual which symbolically brings a person into the Christian Church. Water is used to represent the person's "rebirth" and the "washing away" of sins.

Baroque An artistic style first established at the beginning of the 17th century. Represented by works of drama and bold grandeur, it became known for detail, opulence, and sensuality.

Bestial Animal-like; depraved. Either with animal-like habits, violence, or sub-human intelligence.

Blasphemy An act that demonstrates disrespect for God, or something held sacred. It could be something said, written, or acted out.

Cadaver A dead human body; a corpse.

Caul The amniotic sac that surrounds a baby when it is in the womb. There are many superstitions about babies born with the caul still on, including, it is thought, putting the baby at risk of becoming a vampire.

Coagulation The clotting of the blood when exposed to air.

Consecrated Blessed for ritual purpose. Most often used to either describe the Eucharist or a burial ground such as a churchyard. Burial in unconsecrated ground was considered a punishment for suicides, witches, the un-Christened, and the excommunicated.

Contagion The spread of disease, such as a plague, throughout a population.

Daywalker Either a vampire who is able to walk in daylight, or a dhampir or other half-vampire who has some attributes of vampirism, but is able to walk about in sunlight.

Decadence State of lowered moral standards associated with extravagant behavior and self-indulgence.

Decapitation The removal of the head; beheading. This is one method considered very effective for killing a vampire.

Deity A god, goddess, or other divine being, or someone who is treated like a god.

Dhampir A half-human/half-vampire. The dhampir is someone born into the condition. They can either be conceived between a vampire and a non-vampire, or be *in utero* when their mother is turned into a vampire. They tend to have the strengths of vampires without the weaknesses.

Dogma A fixed set of beliefs held up as undeniably true by a religious or moral group.

Donor One who willingly allows their blood to be drunk by a vampire.

Esoteric Hidden, or secret, something which does not make sense to the majority of people, or is only intended for a select audience.

Etymology The study of the origins and development of words.

Eucharist Also known as Mass or Communion, it is the symbolic, sacramental eating of bread and drinking of wine to represent Jesus's body and blood in Christian Churches. In some traditions the blessed Communion wafers are considered a vampire-repellent.

Excommunication Being formally banned from a place of worship. Though not necessarily a permanent ban, this is seen to reduce significantly a person's chances of getting to Heaven, and also means the person cannot be buried in consecrated ground.

Exhumation The digging up and removal of a body from its grave. Those who were suspected of being vampires would sometimes be exhumed to confirm whether or not they were a vampire, and be killed if they were.

Exorcism The process of driving a demon out of a possessed person. Usually carried out by a member of the clergy.

Ghoul An evil spirit or, in Islamic tradition, a demon that snatches recently buried bodies and attacks children and travelers.

Glamor An illusory attractiveness; a magical spell to make someone seem more attractive.

Gothic An Ancient East Germanic people, a revived medieval architectural style, or relating to a genre of fiction that focuses on the gloomy, horrific, grotesque, and mysterious. Examples might include *Dracula, Frankenstein*, the *Tale of Dr Jeckyll and Mr Hide*, and the *Picture of Dorian Grey*.

Goth A person who belongs to the Goth subculture. Interests include gothic literature, dark or historical clothing, and usually certain types of music.

Grimoire A magician's book for calling up spirits.

Hallowed Sacred or holy.

Hammer Horror The horror movies produced by the UK-based Hammer Film Productions company. The company is best known for its low-budget, but visually ambitious, often grizzly, films produced from the 1950s to the 1970s.

Hereditary Passed from one generation on to the next one.

Heretic A person who believes something different to the Church's teachings, but still claims to be of that religion.

Immortality To be able to live forever, unable to die. Sometimes taken to mean "unable to die of natural causes," so although a vampire cannot die of disease or starvation, it can be killed with sunlight or violent methods.

Inauspicious Ill-fated, signifying bad luck or lack of success.

Incubus A male demon that has sex with women while they sleep.

Interred Buried in the ground.

Japanese Lolita A fashion movement started in the 1980s influenced by Victorian styles and clothing and characterized by bows, bell-shaped skirts, and knee-length socks.

Mary Sue A term referring to a character who can do everything; who charges into the story and solves all the problems. The Sue, as she is often called, usually acts as an idealized and unrealistic self-insertion into the story. The term originated from Lieutenant Mary Sue in a parody *Star Trek* tale written in 1973 to poke fun at fan fiction writers whose characters were wish-fulfilment fantasies. The male version is variously referred to as Marty or Gary Stu.

Master A vampire with human thralls or who has created further vampires that remain under its control. *See Thralls.*

Mausoleum A large tomb or a building in a graveyard made to entomb several bodies above the ground, each in its own compartment.

Monotheistic Believing in one single god.

Necromancer A sorcerer.

New Romantic A fashion movement popular in the UK in the 1980s characterized by frilly shirts and dramatic makeup for men and women and associated with bands such as Spandau Ballet, Adam and the Ants, and Duran Duran.

Nosferatu The word "nosferatu" literally means "undead." However it is also the name of two iconic movies featuring a pale bald-headed Dracula figure with sharp, pointed fingers, ears and teeth, and so has come to mean a particular representation of vampires.

Thrall One enslaved or indentured to a vampire by a blood or psychic link, or one who simply loves the vampire so much that they will do its bidding.

Patriarchal Relating to a group or society where men are the most powerful.

Penny Dreadful The cheap, sensationalist Victorian horror books, which would be serialized and sold for one penny per chapter.

Plague The spread of a highly infectious, usually fatal, disease. The bubonic plague (Black Death) is sometimes referred to as the Great Plague.

Predator An animal that lives off other animals, hunting and killing them. It also suggests a certain amount of enjoyment of the process of the chase and the kill.

REM/Rapid Eye Movement A stage of sleep, where the mind is dreaming and the eyes move about rapidly under the eyelids. The rest of the body is paralyzed to stop the person from acting out their dreams.

Revenant Literally means "returning" in French—used to describe one returning from the grave. This could either mean that they have risen again as something undead, or that they were not actually dead in the first place.

Selkie A mythical creature of Scottish origin, usually female. Selkies live in the sea in the form of seals, but come on land and take off their skins in order to dance or sunbathe. If a human can steal the skin, he can keep the selkie captive. There are legends of men marrying selkies and having families, but life on land is stifling for the creature, and she often becomes weak and frail. If she can find her sealskin, she will immediately return to the sea.

Sorcery Refers to magic with a bad intent: hexes, black magic, and spells cast to do another harm.

Splatterpunk A genre of horror-writing typified by ultra violence, vicious sex, and vast amounts of gore. It's designed as a reaction to and against traditional horror stories, where the horror is suggested rather than described. It can occasionally be so over-the-top that it numbs the reader's mind, thus defeating its own purpose.

Succubus A female demon that has sex with men while they sleep.

Supernatural Forces which exist outside of the natural and scientifically explainable world.

Telepathic Able to understand others' thoughts or feelings, or communicate with them mentally, without using words or signals.

Unconsecrated *See Consecrated.*

Underworld A series of movies in which vampires and werewolves are at war in a contemporary urban setting.

Vampyre Someone who chooses to live in a lifestyle reminiscent of a vampire.

Werewolf A human who turns into a wolf. In most stories the change usually happens during a full Moon, against the person's will. Often the werewolf has supernatural strength.

Bibliography

FICTION

Chetwynd-Hayes, Ronald *The Monster Club*, London, NEL Books, 1981

Elrod, P.N. *The Vampire Files*, New York, Ace Books, 1990

Fortune, Dion *The Demon Lover*, London, Star Books, 1976

Hambly, Barbara *Immortal Blood*, London, Unwin Books, 1988

Hambly, Barbara *Travelling with the Dead*, London, Voyager, 1995

Hamilton, Laurell K. *Guilty Pleasures*, London, Orbit, 2005

Harris, Charlaine *Dead Until Dark*, New York, Ace Books, 2001

Huff, Tanya *Blood Price*, London, Orbit, 1991

Huff, Tanya *Blood Trail*, London, Orbit, 1992

Huff, Tanya *Blood Pact*, London, Orbit, 1993

Huff, Tanya *Blood Lines*, London, Orbit, 1992

Meyer, Stephenie *Twilight*, London, Atom Books, 2008

Meyer, Stephenie *New Moon*, London, Atom Books, 2009

Rice, Anne *Interview with the Vampire*, London, Futura Books, 1988

Rice, Anne *The Vampire Lestat*, London, Futura Books, 1985

Rice, Anne *Queen of the Damned*, London, Futura Books, 1988

Ryan, Alan (ed.) *The Penguin Book of Vampire Stories*, London, Penguin, 1988

Stoker, Bram *Dracula*, London, Arrow Books, 1973

Taylor, Joules *Haadri: Prime Contact*, Bristol, Heartsown, 2008

Vaughn, Carrie *Kitty and the Midnight Hour*, New York, Warner Books, 2005

Warrington, Freda *A Taste of Blood Wine*, London, Pan, 1992

Warrington, Freda *A Dance in Blood Velvet*, New York, Tor Books, 1994

Warrington, Freda *The Dark Blood of Poppies*, London, Pan, 1995

Yarbro, Chelsea Quinn *Hotel Transylvania*, London, NEL Books, 1978

Yarbro, Chelsea Quinn *Blood Games*, New York, Tor Books, 1980

NON-FICTION

Frayling, Christopher (ed.) *Vampyres: Lord Byron to Count Dracula*, London, Faber and Faber, 1992

Hill, Douglas *Return from the Dead*, London, Macdonald, 1970

Masters, Anthony *The Natural History of the Vampire*, Mayflower Books, 1975

Melton, J. Gordon *The Vampire Book: Encyclopedia of the Undead*, Michigan, Visible Ink Books, 1999

Page, Carol *Blood Lust: Conversations with Real Vampires*, London, HarperCollins, 1991

Summers, Montague *The Vampire*, New York, Dorset Books, 1991

Summers, Montague *The Vampire in Europe*, CT, Bracken Books, 1996

Taylor, Ken *Dartmouth Ghosts and Mysteries*, Dartmouth, Richard Webb Publications, 2006

Further Reading

There is a huge range of vampire books available. The ones listed here are not necessarily particularly well written and won't appeal to everyone, but they do present their vampires in a slightly unusual way.

Arthur, Keri *Kissing Sin*, London, Piatkus Books, 2007
Riley Jenson, a werewolf with a touch of vampire, is an agent working for the Directorate of Other Races, an organization set up to police supernatural creatures in Melbourne, Australia.

Bergstrom, Elaine *The Austra Family Chronicles (series)*, New York, Ace Books, 1994
The Austras are a family of hereditary vampires, able to have children, although the ability comes at a price. An intriguing glimpse into a different sort of world.

Charnas, Suzy McKee *The Vampire Tapestry*, London, Granada Paperback, 1980.
The story of anthropologist, dream researcher and vampire Dr Edward Lewis Weyland's journey to an understanding of the creatures he hunts.

Daniels, Les *The Don Sebastian Vampire Chronicles (series)*, London, Raven Books, 1994
The adventures of a vampire through history. Similar in concept to the Saint Germain Chronicles but considerably more gory, fantastic and much less believable.

Hendee, Barb and J.C. *The Noble Dead* series of books, London, Orbit, 2005 onward.
The complex, epic tale of the dhampir Magiere, her half-elf lover Leesil, and the dog-like fey Chap as they search for Magiere's past and Leesil's future in an alternative Medieval Earth.

Henrick, Richard *Vampire in Moscow*, Lake Geneva, USA TSR Inc, 1988
Since Roman times a special sect of warriors has been waiting, pledged to battle the Evil One. Two thousand years later, an alliance of American and Soviet warriors battle the undead menace following the precepts of St John the Pursuer. Interesting concept, and effectively portrayed.

King, Stephen *Salem's Lot*, London, New English Library, 1989
Vampires in Maine. Stephen King's ever-popular, classic, masterful tale, made into two TV mini-series, in 1979 and 2004.

Lumley, Brian *The Necroscope Chronicles*, London, Grafton Books, 1986 onward
Massive, intricate, richly-told multi-part epic set in two different continua, Earth and a world ruled by Wamphyri (alien vampires) reached through the Möebius continuum.

Martin, George R.R. *Fever Dream*, London, Sphere Books Ltd, 1983
Set in the second half of the 19th century. Vampires along the Mississippi: the good, who survive on a blood substitute, and the bad, who prefer to take their sustenance the old-fashioned way. Human-vampire friendship and trust, and a new vampire mythology. A fascinating read.

Newman, Kim *Anno Dracula*, London, Pocket Books, 1993
A parallel world in which vampires live and work among humans. In 1888 Queen Victoria married Count Dracula, opening the way for an influx of the undead. Plot revolves around the murders of vampire prostitutes

in Whitechapel, London. The novel has a huge cast of both fictional and historical characters and is satisfyingly complex.

YOUNG ADULT VAMPIRE FICTION

Caine, Rachel, *The Morganville Vampires (series)*, London, Allison and Busby, 2006–
Claire Danvers is the youngest girl in college and the smartest, which doesn't endear her at all to her schoolmates, especially the college "queen" Monica and her acolytes. Fearing for her safety, Claire moves off campus into a room in an imposing old house. But her new housemates have their own secrets not helped by the fact that the town seems to be ruled by vampires.

Duval, Alex, *Vampire Beach (series)*, New York, Random House, 2006–
When Jason and his sister move to Malibu, the last thing they expect to find is that the town is full of vampires. These vampires are the elite, rich, powerful, and beautiful, especially Sienna Devereux, who catches Jason's eye and are also benign, living on blood but not killing for it. It's a very interesting place to live but of course, things do not run smoothly for very long...

Mead, Richelle, *Vampire Academy (series)*, London, Puffin Books, 2007–
Rose is a dhampir, best friend to the Moroi (mortal) vampire princess, Lissa. St. Vladimir's Academy is a college where Rose is being trained to become Lissa's guardian. But Lissa has unique powers that are desired by the Strigoi, the true immortal and nasty vampires, and they will stop at nothing to own her.

Schrieber, Ellen, *Vampire Kisses (series)*, HarperCollins, 2005–
Sixteen-year-old Raven, self-imposed outcast and goth, has always wanted to be a vampire. Then the Sterling family move into town, and the teenage son Alexander, as well as being gorgeous, also acts suspiciously like a vampire. The series of books charts their tempestuous ongoing relationship.

Smith L.J., *The Vampire Diaries (series)*, London, Harper Books, 1991
The story of Stephan and Damon, ancient vampire brothers, one trying to coexist with humans, the other true to his vampiric nature, and Elena, the human beauty who Stephan loves. But Damon must have everything his brother wants...

Wilde, Terry Lee, *The Vampire... In My Dreams*, Macon, GA, Samhain Publishing, 2008
Witch Marissa falls for fledgling vampire Dominic, but the centuries-old vampire Lynetta wants him for herself...

Other Resources

Fright Night *(movie)*
Released 1985
Director: Tom Holland
Actors: Chris Sarandon, William Ragsdale,
Amanda Bearse, Roddy McDowall

When vampire-mad student Charley Brewster discovers his new neighbor is a vampire, the only person who will believe him is Peter Vincent, fearless vampire killer and washed-up actor, the host of Fright Night, Charley's favorite TV show.

A cult movie, with early but interesting vampire special effects and a very suave, handsome vampire villain. It was successful enough that a very enjoyable sequel was made, with some nice comic touches.

Ultraviolet *(TV series)*
Released: 1998
Director: Joe Ahearne
Actors: Susannah Harker, Jack Davenport, Idris Elba
Philip Quast

Six-part British TV show, a government-funded paramilitary police unit combating the UK part of a global vampire menace. Very high tech, with believable and very dangerous vampires.

ONLINE RESOURCES

Monstropedia
www.monstropedia.org
A sub-section of www.monstrous.com

Fascinating, wide-ranging and detailed exploration of all the popular monsters, including an extensive section on vampires.

Unfortunately few references are given, but it's an excellent starting place for the novice.

Wikipedia
The ever-popular and occasionally extremely useful
www.wikipedia.com

The Internet Movie Database
www.imdb.com

Index

Page numbers in *italics* indicate illustrations and captions. Definite and indefinite articles (A, The) at the beginning of book and movie titles have been ignored. An asterisk (*) indicates the name of a character in a book or movie.

PICTURE CREDITS

AKG 16; 20th Century Fox 112; **Alamy** Interfoto Pressebildagentur 21, 90; J Marshall/Tribal Eye Images 64; Jack Carey 57; Photo 12 98, 101, 109, 117; Pictorial Press 139, 155; **Bridgeman Art Library** Bibliothèque Polonaise 63; **Corbis UK Ltd** Bettmann 52; Christina Simmons 122; Fabian Cevallos/Sygma 37; François Duhamel 11; Harry Briggs 118; Lakesure entertainment/Zuma 55, 115; Peter Endig 121; Sygma 51; **Getty Images** AFP 92; Bridgeman Art Library 58; Christopher Furlong 123; Hulton Archive 78, 95, 107; Hungarian School 111; Time & Life Pictures 137; Warner Bros. 2; **PA Photos** AP 77; **Photo12** Archives du 7eme 13, 42, 72, 93, 96, 105, 132, 158, 170, 171; Collection Cinema 27, 117, 153, 167; **Picture Desk** 81; Orion/Paramount 163; Universal 175; **Rex Features** Everett Collection 7, 29, 136, 157; Warner Bro/Everett 162; **TopFoto** 82, 89; Charles Walker 23; Fortean 66, 85, 143; FotoWare FotoStation 19; Rodger-Vollet 65; **Touchpaper TV** Adrian Rogers 131.